YOUNG ADULT

The ELI Readers collection is a complete range of books and plays for readers of all ages, ranging from captivating contemporary stories to timeless classics. There are three series, each catering for a different age group; Young ELI Readers, Teen ELI Readers and Young Adult ELI Readers. The books are carefully edited and beautifully illustrated to capture the essence of the stories and plots.
The readers are supplemented with 'Focus on' texts packed with background cultural information about the writers and their lives and times.

The FSC certification guarantees that the paper used in these publications comes from certified forests, promoting responsible forestry management worldwide.

For this series of ELI graded readers, we have planted 5000 new trees.

Wilkie Collins

The Woman in White

Retold and Activities by Silvana Sardi
Illustrated by Victoria Semykina

The Woman in White
Wilkie Collins
Retold and Activities: Silvana Sardi
Language Level Consultant: Lisa Suett
Illustrated by Victoria Semykina

ELI Readers
Founder and Series Editors
Paola Accattoli, Grazia Ancillani, Daniele Garbuglia (Art Director)

Graphic Design
Airone Comunicazione - Sergio Elisei

Layout
Airone Comunicazione

Production Manager
Francesco Capitano

Photo credits
Shutterstock

© 2016 ELI s.r.l.
P.O. Box 6
62019 Recanati MC
Italy
T +39 071750701
F +39 071977851
info@elionline.com
www.elionline.com

Typeset in 13 / 18 pt Monotype Dante

Printed in Italy by Tecnostampa Recanati – ERA325.01
ISBN 978-88-536-2110-8

First edition: March 2016

www.eligradedreaders.com

Contents

6	Main Characters	
8	Before you read	
10	Chapter 1	**London – A Strange Meeting**
18	Activities	
20	Chapter 2	**The Marriage Settlement**
28	Activities	
30	Chapter 3	**The Boat-house**
38	Activities	
40	Chapter 4	**Danger at Blackwater Park**
48	Activities	
50	Chapter 5	**Illness and Lies**
58	Activities	
60	Chapter 6	**A Death in London**
68	Activities	
70	Chapter 7	**A Family Secret**
78	Activities	
80	Chapter 8	**Count Fosco's Past Life**
88	Activities	
90	Focus on...	**Wilkie Collins**
92	Focus on...	**CLIL History: Women in the Victorian Age**
94	Test yourself	
95	Syllabus	

These icons indicate the parts of the story that are recorded
start ▶ stop ■

MAIN CHARACTERS

Marian Halcombe

Count Fosco

Sir Percival Glyde

Madame Fosco

Laura Fairlie

Walter Hartright

Anne Catherick

Frederick Fairlie

BEFORE YOU READ

Reading Comprehension – Preliminary

1 Read about *The Woman in White*. Complete the text with the correct word for each space from A, B, C or D.

The Woman in White is a book about mystery and crime. There are _B_ of dark secrets which the reader (**1**) ___ out about as the story (**2**) ___ told. In this kind of book, there is usually a hero, a heroine and a bad person. In The Woman in White, there are two heroines. First, there is Laura who Walter Hartright falls in love (**3**) ___ . She's beautiful and very sweet, but she does almost (**4**) ___ . This was a popular type of woman with English men in the 19th (**5**) ___ . Then there is Laura's sister, Marian, who isn't (**6**) ___ her sister at all. She's very clever, active and not very pretty. She takes (**7**) ___ of Laura and tries to protect her as (**8**) ___ as she can, also with the help of Walter Hartright. Sir Percival Glyde and his friend Count Fosco, are the two people they have to fight against. Count Fosco is very clever and he's (**9**) ___ one who thinks up the plan which could destroy Laura's life forever. Sir Percival Glyde isn't as clever as his friend, but he is just as bad as Count Fosco and will do anything to get his hands on Laura's money. Finally, there is the 'Woman in White'. She hates Sir Percival Glyde but you'll have to read the story to discover (**10**) ___ .

	A	B	C	D
	A many	**B lots**	C very	D much
1	A takes	B goes	C finds	D brings
2	A is	B was	C will	D has
3	A to	B at	C from	D with
4	A something	B everything	C nothing	D anything
5	A year	B time	C century	D age
6	A so	B like	C as	D alike
7	A time	B care	C worry	D trouble
8	A good	B many	C little	D much
9	A that	B this	C the	D which
10	A why	B what	C who	D because

Writing/Speaking

2 Answer the following questions, then compare them with a partner.

1 What kind of books do you like reading? Why?
   _____
   _____

2 How often do you read for pleasure?
   _____
   _____

3 Why do you think e-books have become popular?
   _____
   _____

4 What else do you do in your free time?
   _____
   _____

Listening

▶ 2 **3 Listen to the start of Chapter One and decide if these sentences are true (T) or false (F).**

		T	F
	Walter Hartright was learning to draw.	☐	✓
1	The story starts at the end of July.	☐	☐
2	Walter Hartright had a good job in London.	☐	☐
3	Mr Pesca had just arrived in London.	☐	☐
4	The two men had been friends for a long time.	☐	☐
5	Mr Pesca was a drawing teacher.	☐	☐
6	Mr Pesca had found himself a new job in the country.	☐	☐
7	Two women lived with Frederick Fairlie.	☐	☐
8	Walter Hartright left his mother's home before midnight.	☐	☐
9	It wasn't cold that night.	☐	☐
10	Walter Hartright met a woman dressed in white.	☐	☐

Chapter 1

London –
A Strange Meeting

▶ 2

THE STORY BEGUN
BY WALTER HARTRIGHT –
DRAWING TEACHER.

Sometimes the police don't always discover crimes. The story of this crime is told for the first time in these pages. Walter Hartright, twenty-eight years old and a drawing teacher, will begin the story.

It was the last day of July. After a long hot summer, I found myself in London with no job and no money. One evening I went to visit my sister and mother in Hampstead. My old Italian friend, Mr Pesca was there too. He had left Italy many years ago and now taught languages in London. I had saved his life once in the sea at Brighton a long time ago, and we had become great friends.

'I've found you a job in a rich country house,' said Mr Pesca. 'You'll teach two lovely ladies how to draw.'

I'd work for a rich businessman, Frederick Fairlie of Limmeridge House, Cumberland. He wanted me to start immediately. I thanked my dear friend and spent the rest of the evening with him and my family.

It was almost midnight when I started walking back to my flat in London. I was enjoying the peace and quiet of that warm night when suddenly my heart almost stopped – somebody had touched me on

THE WOMAN IN WHITE

the shoulder. I turned round. There, in the middle of the road was a woman dressed from head to foot in white.

▶ 3 'Is this the road to London?' she asked.

I looked at her carefully. Her face was very pale*. She was young and thin and had long, fair hair. There was nothing wild about her. She was quiet.

'Did you hear me?' she said, still quietly and quickly. 'I asked you if this was the way to London.'

'Yes, sorry,' I said. 'This is the right road. I was just a bit surprised to see you.'

'You don't think I've done anything wrong, do you?' she said. 'I've done nothing wrong. I've met with an accident.'

'Please, believe me, I don't think you've done anything wrong,' I said. 'Tell me how I can help you.'

'Can I get a carriage*?' she said. 'Is it too late? I've a friend in London. Will you promise to let me leave you when you find me a carriage?'

'Yes,' I said.

We started walking together towards London. Suddenly she asked:

'Do you know many important people in London?'

'Yes, why?'

'Because I hope that there's one important person you don't know.'

'Will you tell me his name?'

'I can't – don't ask me to talk about him!' she said angrily.

I could see she was upset so I decided to change the subject.

'I'm a drawing teacher,' I said. 'Tomorrow I'm leaving London to go and work in Cumberland.'

pale without colour   **carriage**

11

'Cumberland!' she said. 'I wish I was going there too. I was once happy there. I was born in Hampshire, but I went to school in Cumberland for a short time. I'd love to see Limmeridge House again.'

I couldn't believe it and stopped suddenly. She had just mentioned Mr Fairlie's house.

'Is there anything wrong?' she asked.

'No, it's just that some people from Cumberland mentioned Limmeridge House to me a few days ago,' I said.

'Ah! Not my people,' she answered. 'Mrs Fairlie is dead – and her husband too; and their little girl may be married and gone away by this time.'

We could see the lights and the houses of the city now. A carriage stopped to let some people out. The woman ran towards the carriage and got in it. She took my hand and kissed it as the carriage drove away. The woman in white was gone. Suddenly I heard the wheels of another carriage. It stopped and two men spoke to a police officer.

'Have you seen a woman in white?' said one of the men.

'No,' answered the police officer. 'Why are you looking for her?'

'She's escaped from my Asylum*!' said the other man.

Escaped from an Asylum! She had seemed a little strange but not mad. I got home but couldn't sleep. I kept thinking about the woman in white. Would we meet again?

Morning came and I left for Cumberland. I arrived at Limmeridge House late that night. When I got up the next morning, it was a beautiful sunny day and I could see the sea from my window. I went downstairs for breakfast and met one of my pupils, Miss Marian Halcombe. She was a young dark-haired woman, not very pretty, but tall and slim.

'I'm afraid it's just the two of us for breakfast,' she said. 'My sister, Miss Fairlie, has a headache and my uncle, Mr Fairlie never has his

---

Asylum a special hospital for people with mental illness meals with us. He stays in his room all the time as he thinks he's always ill. Actually Mr Fairlie isn't really my uncle and Miss Fairlie isn't really my sister.'

'Sorry, I don't understand,' I said.

'I'll explain,' she said smiling. 'My mother was married twice. The first time to Mr Halcombe, my father, the second time to Mr Philip Fairlie, my half-sister's father. Now our parents are all dead. My father was a poor man and Miss Fairlie's father was rich. Everybody thinks I'm strange, and everybody thinks she's sweet and charming. Mr Frederick Fairlie, who you'll meet later, is Mr Philip Fairlie's younger brother; he isn't married and he's Miss Fairlie's guardian*. I won't live without Miss Fairlie and she can't live without me – and that's why I'm at Limmeridge House. Even if we're so different, we're very fond of each other. Will you manage to accept a quiet, country life or will you secretly wish for a change and adventure?'

'I had an adventure, before coming here,' I said. I then told her about my meeting with the woman in white. She was interested and surprised to hear that the woman in white had spoken kindly about Mrs Fairlie, her mother.

'I wish we knew her name,' she said. 'We must try and solve this mystery. Don't tell Mr Fairlie or my sister yet; they'd get worried. After her second marriage, my mother started the village school, but the old teachers are all dead. However, I have the letters she wrote to my father. I'll look at them this morning while you're with Mr Fairlie. I'll see you for lunch at 2 p.m., Mr Hartright, and you'll meet my sister too. Till then goodbye.'

I saw Mr Fairlie for not more than 10 minutes. He was too tired and nervous to talk to me. He was a horrible man. I met Miss Fairlie after lunch in the garden. How can I describe Laura Fairlie as she was

guardian a person who by law looks after a young person

then before everything that has happened since that happy moment? She was a young, slim girl with long fair hair and light blue eyes. A fair, delicate* girl, in a pretty, light dress. She was the most beautiful girl I had ever seen.

After a long pleasant drive in the countryside, I met the two ladies again that evening for dinner. Miss Fairlie was wearing a simple white dress. I later found out that she always dressed in a simple way because she didn't want to seem richer than Miss Halcombe. After dinner, Miss Fairlie went out into the garden. I was just going to join her when Miss Halcombe called me. She had found something interesting in one of her mother's letters.

'Listen,' she said. 'Here my mother is speaking about the school. She says:

Dear Philip,

Mrs Kempe is very ill so her sister from Hampshire, Mrs Catherick, has come to look after her. She has a sweet little girl. She's about a year older than our dear Laura. Her name's Anne and she's going to come and do lessons. Anne is eleven years old but she's a little slow. The doctor saw her but thinks she'll improve, as she grows up. Although she's slow, once she has an idea in her head she never forgets it. She's so sweet, I gave her some of Laura's old white dresses and hats. She said: 'I'll always wear white as long as I live. It'll help me to remember you.' Now my love, the most surprising thing: although Anne Catherick isn't half so pretty, she has the same hair, colour of eyes and shape of face as –'

'Miss Fairlie!' I said. She was standing in the garden looking towards us. She really looked like the woman in white! So, Anne Catherick was the woman I had met on the road to London!

'You see it now, as my mother saw it eleven years ago!' said Miss Halcombe. 'Let's keep this a secret between you and me for now.'

delicate not strong, easily broken

The days and weeks passed happily. I taught my pupils to draw and enjoyed being with them. Miss Halcombe had become a great friend and Miss Fairlie? I think you can guess. I was in love with Miss Fairlie! Of course I never said anything and neither did she, but it was obvious to everybody that we enjoyed being with each other. Then everything changed.

One morning, I went down to breakfast. The ladies hadn't arrived yet. Then Miss Halcombe came in, followed by Miss Fairlie. They seemed worried.

'Sorry,' said Miss Halcombe, 'I was talking to Mr Fairlie.' Miss Fairlie didn't look at me. Her face was very pale. Then Miss Halcombe said:

'I've seen your uncle, Laura. He thinks we should get the purple room ready; and Monday is the day – not Tuesday.'

Miss Fairlie said nothing. She just looked down at the table. Then she stood up, looked at me sadly* and I knew I'd lose her soon.

'Mr Hartright,' said Miss Halcombe, 'get your hat and come out to the garden. I need to speak to you in private.'

I followed her out to the garden.

'Mr Hartright,' she said, 'during your time here, we've become friends. I liked you immediately for the way you were kind to the woman in white.'

These words made me suddenly think of my adventure again on the road to London.

'As your friend,' she continued, 'I'm going to tell you that I've discovered your secret. You're in love with my sister, Laura. I'm sorry that you've opened your heart to a hopeless love.'

She took my hand and at that moment, I wanted to cry.

'Listen to me,' she said softly. 'You must leave Limmeridge House, Mr Hartright, before you hurt each other even more. You

---

sadly not happily

15

must leave because Laura Fairlie is engaged to be married to a rich man called Sir Percival Glyde, from Hampshire. You must leave, not just for yourself but also for her. I, who love her more than my own life, know how miserable she has been since she felt this love for you. She doesn't love her future husband. Her father made her promise on his death-bed two years ago. Till you came here, she was the same as hundreds of other women, who marry men without liking or disliking them, and who learn to love or hate them after marriage. I know you'll understand how important it is for you to go away so that my sister can find peace again. Be kind to her like you were with the stranger on the road.'

Hampshire! Where Anne Catherick was born. She had been afraid of a rich man from Hampshire. I had the feeling that there was something dangerous about Miss Fairlie's future, but all I said was:

'Tell me when to go. I'll do anything you ask.'

Just then, a servant* arrived.

'Please, Miss Halcombe, Miss Fairlie wants you. She's very upset about a letter she's received,' said the servant.

I went back to my room to pack my bags, and Miss Halcombe went to her sister.

---

servant somebody who works for a person in their house

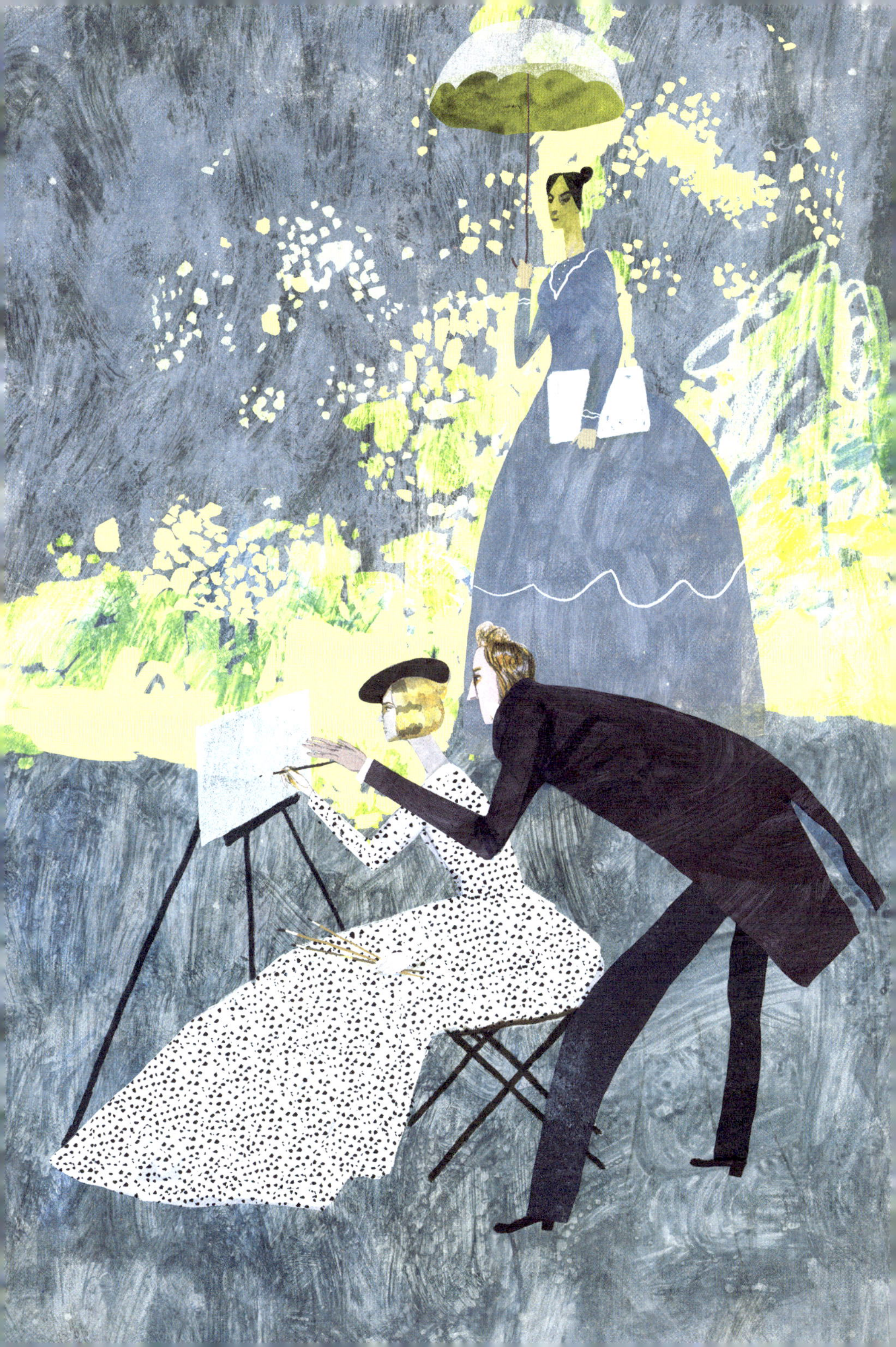

AFTER-READING ACTIVITIES

Stop & Check

1 Choose the correct answer, A, B or C about Chapter One.

Once, Walter Hartright had saved Mr Pesca's life in
- A London.
- B Hampstead.
- C Brighton.

1 The woman in white on the road to London was
- A quiet.
- B old.
- C wild.

2 The woman in white said
- A she had done something wrong.
- B she had a friend in London.
- C she wanted Hartright to go in the carriage with her.

3 The woman in white knew Cumberland because
- A she was born there.
- B she had gone to school there.
- C she lived there now with her family.

4 One of the men spoke to the police officer because
- A the woman worked for him in his Asylum.
- B the woman had left her bag in his Asylum.
- C the woman had escaped from his Asylum.

5 Miss Halcombe and Miss Fairlie had
- A the same mother.
- B the same colour of hair.
- C the same father.

6 Walter Hartright realised that Miss Fairlie looked like
- A Miss Halcombe.
- B her uncle.
- C Anne Catherick.

7 Miss Halcombe told Hartright to leave Limmeridge House because
- A he wasnt a good drawing teacher.
- B she was in love with him.
- C Laura Fairlie was engaged to be married to a rich man.

Vocabulary

2 Complete the sentences with a verb from the box in the correct form. The verb may be affirmative or negative.

> love • ~~have~~ • be • live • wear • arrive • walk • find

At the end of summer, Walter Hartright _didn't have_ a job or any money.
1. Before becoming a teacher in England, Mr Pesca _____ in Italy.
2. As he _____ home, Walter Hartright met a woman dressed in white.
3. If she had the chance, the woman in white _____ to see Limmeridge House again.
4. At dinner time, Miss Fairlie _____ a simple white dress.
5. One evening, Miss Halcombe _____ something interesting in her mother's letters.
6. One morning, Walter Hartright went down to breakfast but the ladies _____ yet.
7. Laura Fairlie _____ miserable since falling in love with Walter.

PRE-READING ACTIVITY

Listening

▶ 4 **3** Listen to the beginning of Chapter Two and complete the sentences with the words you hear.

The letter Laura received had no _name_ on it.
1. Sir Percival seemed very _____ and charming.
2. Mr Hartright is going to go abroad to try and _____ Laura.
3. Laura would never break the _____ she made to her father.
4. Miss Halcombe told Mr Hartright about the _____ before he left.
5. Mr Hartright keeps thinking about Anne Catherick's _____.
6. Anne Catherick was _____ of a rich man from Hampshire.
7. Mr Hartright is worried about Laura's _____ with Sir Percival Glyde.

Chapter 2

*The Marriage Settlement**

▶ 4   THE STORY CONTINUED BY MISS HALCOMBE.

I don't know what to think any more. The letter Laura received had no name on it but it said a lot of bad things about her future husband, Sir Percival Glyde. Then, he came to stay for a few days and seemed very kind and charming. Mr Hartright has gone. He was so upset, and Laura too. He's going to go abroad to try and forget her. It's best for both of them. Laura would never break the promise she made to her father to marry Sir Percival Glyde. I told Mr Hartright about the letter before he left. He keeps thinking about Anne Catherick's words. She said she was frightened of a rich man from Hampshire. Maybe it's because Anne Catherick and Laura look like each other; maybe it's simply because he's in love with Laura, but Mr Hartright is worried about Laura's future with Sir Percival Glyde.

▶ 5   Mr Gilmore, the family lawyer, is coming tomorrow to speak to Mr Fairlie because Sir Percival Glyde wants to marry Laura before the end of the year. They're going to discuss Laura's marriage settlement. She'll have a lot of money when she's twenty-one on her next birthday. It's late and I'm tired with all these thoughts. Maybe things will seem better tomorrow.

settlement a document to decide about money

This morning I got a letter from Walter Hartright and now I'm even more afraid for Laura than before. Before leaving for London, he met Anne Catherick with her friend, Mrs Clements at Limmeridge church. Anne said she had written the letter to Laura about her future husband. She got very angry when Mr Hartright mentioned Sir Percival's name, but she ran away before Mr Hartright could ask her any more questions. I'm going to speak to Mr Gilmore about the letter as soon as he arrives.

THE STORY CONTINUED BY VINCENT GILMORE – LAWYER.

I arrived at Limmeridge House on Friday, 2nd November. Miss Fairlie didn't look well. I saw Mr Fairlie on Saturday. As usual, he only wanted to talk about himself and his illnesses. As for his niece, he totally agreed with the plans for Laura's marriage to Sir Percival Glyde. Miss Fairlie's father had wanted it and he wanted it too. As her guardian, he believed Miss Fairlie was doing the right thing. I met Sir Percival Glyde on Monday. He seemed a very pleasant man though rather older than I had expected. He's forty-five while Miss Fairlie is only twenty. I've known Miss Fairlie since she was a child and I was worried about her because she seemed uneasy* with her future husband even if he was polite and kind to her.

Miss Halcombe showed me the letter Miss Fairlie had received about her husband. I showed it to Sir Percival Glyde. Sir Percival told us that Mrs Catherick had worked for his family many years ago. The woman had a daughter, Anne who, simply speaking, was a bit mad. Mrs Catherick needed help. Her husband had left her and she didn't have enough money to pay for special care for her daughter.

uneasy not happy, worried

Sir Percival Glyde kindly offered to pay for the Asylum for Anne. Mrs Catherick was very glad of his help, but Anne Catherick had never forgiven Sir Percival. She was too ill to realise that he had done it for her own good. That explained why she had written all those bad things about him in the letter to Miss Fairlie. I was very satisfied with this explanation. Sir Percival even told Miss Halcombe to write to Mrs Catherick to ask her for more details. Miss Halcombe wrote the letter immediately in front of us. Sir Percival didn't even look at the letter. He simply asked:

'Did Anne Catherick see Miss Fairlie?'

'Certainly not!' replied Miss Halcombe.

'It's our duty to find the poor girl,' continued Sir Percival Glyde, 'before she hurts herself or anyone else.'

Mrs Catherick's reply arrived two days later, confirming* Sir Percival's story. I went to see Miss Fairlie to talk to her about her money and the marriage settlement. I explained what she'd have when she became twenty-one, and then when her uncle died.

'May I leave all my money and all my property* to Marian, Mr Gilmore?' asked Laura. 'Don't let him take Marian away from me!'

She started to cry. I had never seen her so sad before. She had always been such a happy child. I left her – she was too nervous to talk about anything. A week after my return to London, I received a letter from Miss Halcombe. It said that Miss Fairlie had decided to do what Sir Percival Glyde wanted and marry him before the end of the year, probably in December. Miss Fairlie wouldn't be twenty-one until after the wedding, at the end of March of the following year.

I must explain about the marriage settlement, as it's a very serious part of Miss Fairlie's story. On her twenty-first birthday, she would get property that would give her £3000 a year. If she died before her

---

confirm say something is true

property land and buildings that belong to a person

husband, Sir Percival would get this money. Apart from this £3000, on Mr Frederick Fairlie's death, Sir Percival and his wife would also become the owners of Limmeridge House. However, the thing that worried me most was another £20,000 that Miss Fairlie's father had left her, and which she would get on her twenty-first birthday. Laura's father had also left £10,000 pounds to his sister, Eleanor, Laura's aunt, which she would get when Laura died. Laura's father, Mr Philip Fairlie had loved his sister, Eleanor, until she had married an Italian man called Count Fosco. Laura's father hated foreigners so he didn't want to leave anything to his sister when he died. In the end, he left her £10,000 that she would only get once Laura was dead. Considering that Eleanor, now Madame Fosco, was much older than her niece, Laura, there wasn't much chance of her ever getting the £10,000. The money for Eleanor was, of course of no interest to Sir Percival. Instead, the £20,000 that Laura would get on her twenty-first birthday was of great interest to him. This would be his wife's own money and she could do what she wanted with it. Therefore, in the marriage settlement, I said that the £20,000 should be Lady Laura Glyde's and only hers until her death and she could choose who to leave this money to. However, Sir Percival's lawyer didn't agree with this last part. On Laura's death, he wanted the £20,000 to go to Sir Percival Glyde and only to him. I tried to talk to Mr Frederick Fairlie about it, since he was Laura's guardian, and she couldn't decide for herself until she was twenty-one. I had found out that Sir Percival Glyde had a lot of debts*, but Mr Fairlie wasn't interested. As usual, he was only worried about the many illnesses he thought he had. In the end, I had to write the marriage settlement saying that, on Laura's death, Sir Percival would get the £20,000 all to himself. I was angry and sad but there was nothing I could do.

debts money you have to pay to others

THE STORY CONTINUED BY MARIAN HALCOMBE – FROM HER DIARY.

8th November: I received a letter from Walter Hartright but I didn't tell Laura. He was waiting in London to leave for his new job in Central America. He hadn't seen Anne Catherick since the last time at the church, but he had the feeling that somebody was watching him. I was worried about him and hoped the change would help him to forget Laura. Then, Laura decided to tell Sir Percival that she was in love with another man, without mentioning Walter Hartright's name. She thought that Sir Percival would be so angry that he wouldn't want to marry her any more. She was wrong! He said:

'I wish to marry you even more, now that you've shown me what an honest woman you are!'

'But I can't give you my love,' said Laura.

'It's enough for me that you'll never see this other man again,' said Sir Percival. With these words, he kissed her hand and left the room. Laura cried and cried – there was nothing more she could do.

'You write to Walter, and he writes to you, Marian,' she said. 'While I'm alive, always tell him I'm well, and never say I'm not happy. If I die first, give him this little book of his drawings and say – Oh, Marian, say I loved him!'

I sat with her for a long time until she was calm again. After that day, she never mentioned Walter Hartright again. She said nothing when Sir Percival decided their wedding date for 22nd December. They're going to get married at Limmeridge Church. After the wedding, they're going to Italy.

17th December: Sir Percival arrived today with some beautiful presents for Laura. Laura never wants to be alone. She wants me to

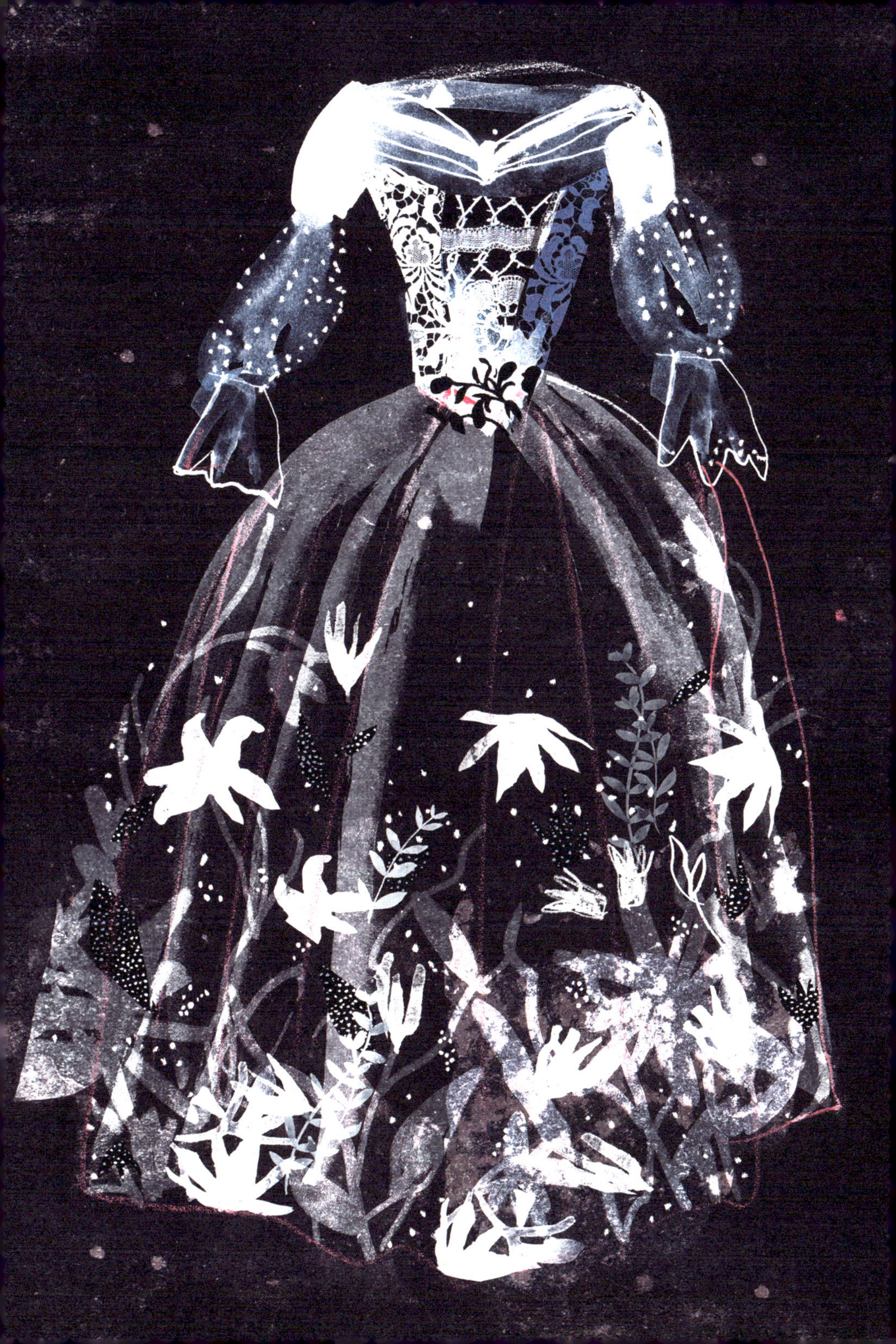

stay with her all the time. When she's with Sir Percival she talks and talks. That's not like her at all. He thinks it's because she's excited about the wedding.

19th December: Maybe I've been wrong about Sir Percival. Maybe he isn't so bad. Today I asked him if I could stay with them after they came back from Italy. He immediately said he had wanted to ask me the same thing and that he'd be glad to have me at Blackwater Park, his home in Hampshire. He also told me that when they are abroad, they'll meet Count Fosco and his wife. Laura hasn't seen her Aunt Eleanor for years. Maybe this is the chance for Madame Fosco and Laura to become friends again since Count Fosco and Sir Percival are such good friends.

22nd December: Laura got up at seven o'clock. She's calm, calmer than ever. It's now ten o'clock and she's wearing her beautiful white wedding dress. I leave her looking at herself in the mirror. Sir Percival is waiting outside for her.

It's eleven o'clock. It's all over. They're married. Three o'clock, they're gone. I'm blind with crying – I can write no more.

11th June 1850 Blackwater Park, Hampshire. Six long months have passed but tomorrow I'll see Laura again. She and her husband are coming back from Italy with Count Fosco and his wife who are going to stay at Blackwater Park for the summer. I'm already at Blackwater Park. I left Limmeridge yesterday, slept in London last night and didn't get here till late this evening. This place is totally different from Limmeridge. It's surrounded by trees. It's all very quiet – too quiet.

I haven't heard from Walter Hartright for months and I know nothing more of Anne Catherick. Mr Gilmore has been unwell and must rest for at least a year. Mr Fairlie is happy to have Limmeridge House to himself now. I've received several letters from Laura but she never says if she's happy or not. When she talks of the future, she never talks about Sir Percival but only about her future as my sister. She says her aunt, Madame Fosco is much nicer than she used to be but she doesn't seem to like Count Fosco.

12th June: I decided to go for a walk today. There's a boat-house near the lake. I found a little dog and took it back to the house because it was bleeding. It died shortly after. When one of the servants saw it, she told me it was Mrs Catherick's dog. Mrs Catherick had come to the house the day before to ask if anyone had seen her daughter, Anne. Somebody had seen a stranger in the area who looked like her daughter. Mrs Catherick lives in Welmingham, quite far from here. Before leaving, she told the servant not to tell Sir Percival that she had come. She also asked a lot of questions about Laura. It's now eight o'clock. They still haven't arrived. I must try and go to Welmingham to meet Mrs Catherick one day. I wish Walter Hartright were here.

AFTER-READING ACTIVITIES

Stop & Check

1 **Match the person to the correct description.**

1. [k] Walter Hartright
2. [ ] Miss Halcombe
3. [ ] Sir Percival Glyde
4. [ ] Mr Gilmore
5. [ ] Frederick Fairlie
6. [ ] Count Fosco
7. [ ] Laura Fairlie
8. [ ] Madame Fosco
9. [ ] Mrs Catherick
10. [ ] Anne Catherick
11. [ ] Philip Fairlie

a is a lawyer.
b lives in Welmingham.
c is Miss Fairlie's aunt.
d is married to Eleanor.
e wants to marry Laura Fairlie.
f wrote terrible things about Sir Percival.
g loves Walter Hartright.
h finds a dog in the boat-house.
i hated foreigners.
j is always worried about his illnesses.
k is going to go abroad.

Preliminary - Writing

2 **You're Anne Catherick. Write a note to Laura Fairlie. In your note you should:**

- tell Laura not to marry Sir Percival
- explain why you hate Sir Percival
- tell her what she should do.

Write 35-45 words.

Grammar - Preliminary

3 **Complete the second sentence so that it means the same as the first. Use no more than 3 words.**

> The letter Laura received had no name on it.
> There _was no name_ on the letter Laura received.

1. Sir Percival Glyde was richer than Walter Hartright.
   Walter Hartright didn't have _____ money as Sir Percival Glyde.
2. Laura would love Walter Hartright until she died.
   Laura would love Walter Hartright as _____ she lived.
3. Sir Percival would get £20,000 if his wife died.
   Until his wife's _____ Sir Percival wouldn't get £20,000.
4. 'Will you come and stay at Blackwater Park, Miss Halcombe?'
   Sir Percival asked Miss Halcombe _____ and stay at Blackwater Park.
5. Laura hasn't seen her Aunt Eleanor for years.
   It's years _____ Laura saw her aunt Eleanor.
6. Blackwater Park is different from Limmeridge.
   Blackwater Park isn't _____ as Limmeridge.
7. Welmingham wasn't very near Blackwater Park.
   Welmingham was quite _____ Blackwater Park.

PRE-READING ACTIVITY

Speaking

4 **Discuss the following questions about Chapter Three with a partner. Then read and see if you guessed right.**

1. Will Laura be happy to see Marian again?
2. Will Laura be glad that she married Sir Percival?
3. Will Marian continue to stay at Blackwater Park?
4. Will Count Fosco and his wife come to Blackwater Park?
5. Will Sir Percival find Anne Catherick?
6. Will Marian meet Mrs Catherick?
7. Will Walter Hartright write to Marian from Central America?

Chapter 3

The Boat-house

▶ 6   THE STORY CONTINUED BY MISS HALCOMBE.

15th June: Two days have passed since the travellers came back. Laura didn't want to talk about her husband. She was just happy to see me again.

'Oh, Marian,' she said suddenly while we were alone. 'Promise you'll never marry, and leave me. Your life is so much better as a single woman – unless you love your husband.'

She stopped, looked down at her hands and said softly:

'Have you written many letters and received many letters recently? Is he well and happy? Has he forgotten me?'

All I could answer was that I hadn't heard from him recently. Now I knew that her heart was still with Walter Hartright. My poor sweet Laura!

Sir Percival seems slimmer and more nervous. He isn't as friendly towards me as before. I don't know what to think of his friend, Count Fosco. He's a very intelligent interesting man. He talks to me seriously as if I were a man. He's about sixty and seems very pleasant but at the same time I feel uneasy with him. He loves his pets. He's got birds and mice which he plays with like a child. Laura was right about her aunt. Madame Fosco has really changed. Before she was the type of woman who complained all the time. Now, at forty-three, she just sits in a corner, says very little and waits for her husband to tell her what to do.

16th June: While we were having lunch, Mr Merriman, Sir Percival's lawyer, arrived at Blackwater Park. Sir Percival seemed surprised and left us sitting at the table. After lunch, I decided to go for a walk. Sir Percival was still with his lawyer in the library. I was going downstairs when the library door opened and I heard the two men talking about Laura. I stopped to listen. They couldn't see me.

'Don't worry, Sir Percival,' said the lawyer. 'All you have to do is tell Lady Glyde to sign the document and your money problems will be over.'

'She'll sign, Mr Merriman. She'll sign,' answered Sir Percival.

I went back to Laura's room and told her everything. She wasn't surprised.

'I know my husband has debts,' said Laura. 'But don't worry, Marian. I won't sign anything without reading it first.'

That evening Sir Percival was much more pleasant to everybody than he had been for the last few days, especially to Laura. Even Madame Fosco looked at him in surprise. This can only mean one thing. I know it, Laura knows and, I'm sure Count Fosco knows why too.

17th June: We all went for a walk to the boat-house. While we were there, Count Fosco saw some blood on the floor. I told them about Mrs Catherick's dog. Sir Percival went back to the house immediately to speak to the servant. When we got back, he was preparing to leave. He was obviously going to Welmingham to see Mrs Catherick.

'I'm sorry to say, I have to leave you,' began Sir Percival, 'a long journey. I'll be back tomorrow but before I go, will you come into the library please, Laura? There's a little business to do. And could you, Count Fosco and your dear wife come too? I need you to see Laura signing a document, nothing more. And of course, you too, Miss Halcombe.'

Laura sat at the table in the library. Count Fosco spoke to me:

'I don't know what this document is about,' he said, 'but I think you and I should see Lady Glyde sign it and not my wife, as she has the same opinion as me. I'm here as the nearest friend of the husband and you, Miss Halcombe, as the nearest friend of the wife. In this way, there'll be no problems in the future.'

Sir Percival put a long document on the table, but only showed Laura the part she had to sign.

'Sign your name here,' said Sir Percival, pointing to the place. 'You and Fosco will sign here afterwards, Miss Halcombe.'

'What am I signing?' asked Laura quietly.

'I have no time to explain,' answered Sir Percival. 'It's only a document, you wouldn't understand. Don't you trust your husband? For the last time, Lady Glyde, will you sign or will you not?'

'Shall I sign Marian?' asked Laura. 'I will, if you tell me.'

'No,' I answered. 'Sign nothing unless you've read it first.'

'Remember you're a guest here, Miss Halcombe!' shouted Sir Percival angrily. 'Never mind your sister, Lady Glyde. Sign!'

Count Fosco put one of his hands on Sir Percival's shoulder. 'Control yourself, Percival,' he said. 'Lady Glyde is right. She needs some time to think. She can sign tomorrow, can't she?'

The two men looked at each other for a long moment. Then, without saying another word, Sir Percival left the room.

'I'm sorry, ladies, that you've seen Sir Percival at his worst,' said Count Fosco. 'As his friend, I promise you that he'll not behave like this again tomorrow.'

I thanked him – yes thanked him because I now realised that he had some power over Sir Percival. I needed him on my side if I wanted to continue staying at Blackwater Park.

After dinner that evening, Laura and I went for a walk to the lake. We sat down in the boat-house and there, Laura told me what I already knew. She was in an unhappy marriage and worst of all, Sir Percival now knew the name of the man she had loved. It happened when they were in Italy. At a party, a lady had spoken about a young drawing teacher. When she said his name, Walter Hartright, Laura hadn't managed to hide her surprise and Sir Percival had understood immediately.

It was now dark. We stood up to leave when suddenly we saw somebody moving in the dark. Then he or she disappeared. We walked as fast as we could back to the house. I went to the library and found Count Fosco and his wife there so it hadn't been them. Sir Percival hadn't come back from his trip yet, so who had been at the boat-house?

18th June: Laura has lost the little necklace I gave her. She thinks it's at the boat-house so she has gone to look for it. Yesterday, I wrote a letter to Mr Gilmore's partner. I told him about the strange document Sir Percival wanted Laura to sign. I asked him to answer me immediately. Then I put it in the postbag downstairs in the hall. Somebody always takes the post to the village every day. Today, instead of waiting at the house, I decided to walk along the road and meet the carriage that brings the post. The lawyer's letter said Lady Glyde shouldn't sign the document if it says that Sir Percival wants to borrow money from her. If he didn't pay this debt to her in the future, she would lose this money forever. I was so busy reading the letter as I walked back to the house that I didn't notice Count Fosco, until it was too late. He was standing in the road, looking straight at me with the letter in my hand. He was smiling and I knew at that moment that he had read my letter to the lawyer the day before. He said nothing about it and didn't ask any questions about the letter I was holding in my hand. He spoke to me in his usual pleasant way. When we reached the house Sir Percival had just arrived. He saw us and said:

'Where's Lady Glyde? I want to see her in the library in half an hour.'

I left the two men and heard Count Fosco say:

'Percival, I need to talk to you about business, it's important.'

The business, for sure, was about the document Laura had to sign, but I couldn't hear them. I felt sick with fear.

While I was waiting for Laura to come back, the Count came into the room.

'I've got good news for you, Miss Halcombe,' he said pleasantly. 'Percival has changed his mind about the document. Lady Glyde won't have to sign it for the moment. Please tell her. I'm sure she'll be as happy as I see you are.'

He left the room before I had the chance to say anything. I was so tired by all these events that I lay down on the couch and closed my eyes. I woke up when Laura came in to look for me. She seemed frightened.

'What has happened?' I asked.

'Marian! – The person at the lake last night – I've just seen her! I've spoken to her! Anne Catherick!'

I was so shocked I couldn't say a word. We went to Laura's room and she told me everything.

'Look Marian!' said Laura pointing to her necklace. 'She found it on the floor of the boat-house. Oh, she talked in such a strange way,

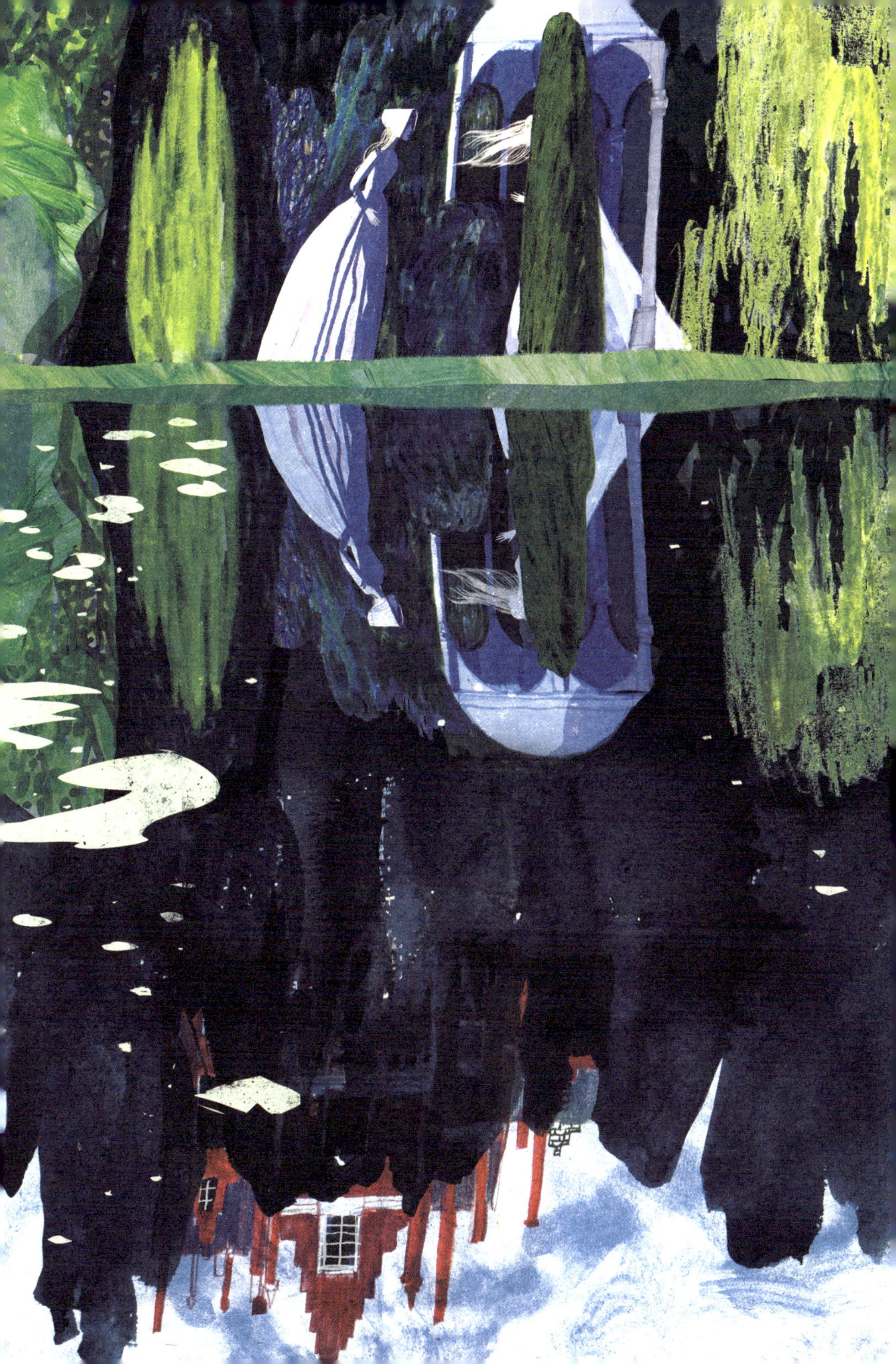

Marian! She looked so ill, and then she left me as suddenly as she had come.'

'Speak low,' I said. 'Remember that Anne Catherick is a dangerous subject under your husband's roof. Start from the beginning and tell me everything.'

'I was looking for the necklace in the boat-house when I heard somebody behind me say "Miss Fairlie", my dear old name. I looked behind me and there she was, a woman in a white dress with an old thin shawl* over it.

She told me that my mother liked her to wear white. Then she asked me if I remembered when we used to walk to school together with my mother. While I was listening to her, I suddenly saw that we looked like each other! Her face was pale and tired – like my face would be after a long illness. I asked her why she had called me "Miss Fairlie". She got very angry and said: "Because I love the name Fairlie and hate the name Glyde!" She hadn't seemed mad till then, but at that moment she was a bit scary. She was the one we heard last night. She listened to us talking. She knows I'm not happy with Sir Percival and she said she was sorry that she hadn't managed to stop the wedding. She said: "I'm so sorry – I only wrote you that letter – I was too frightened to do anything else." I asked her if she was still afraid. Oh Marian! She said she wasn't afraid any more because she was dying! Then she said a very strange thing. She said: "If you know his Secret, he'll be afraid of you; he won't use you as he used me. My mother knows the Secret. She has wasted half her life under the Secret. When I was grown up, she said something to me and the next day your husband…" Then she stopped talking and listened. I asked her to tell me the Secret but she said we weren't alone and told me to come back tomorrow. Then she was gone.'

shawl like a big scarf worn over your shoulders

'Oh Laura, Laura, another chance lost!' I said. 'Did you see or hear anybody else?'

'No,' said Laura.

'Well, tomorrow you must go to the boat-house Laura, but I'll follow you this time.'

'Do you really think there's a Secret my husband is afraid of?'

'Yes, I believe there is,' I replied.

I left Laura and went downstairs to see where Count Fosco and Sir Percival were. I met Madame Fosco and she told me they had gone for a long walk. For a long walk? Neither of them liked walking! I went back upstairs to Laura and told her that Sir Percival didn't want her to sign the document for the moment. Sir Percival and the Count didn't return from their walk until dinner. That evening Sir Percival was polite, especially towards his wife. He was obviously planning something. I'm quite sure he got the information he wanted from Mrs Catherick, when he went to see her. The Count seemed quieter than usual.

Towards midnight everybody started to go to bed. It was now windy outside and it was getting stronger.

'Listen!' the Count said to me. 'There will be a change tomorrow.'

AFTER-READING ACTIVITIES

Stop & Check

1 **Put the sentences about Chapter Three in the right order (1 to 8).**

- [7] The travellers came back to Blackwater Park.
- **A** ☐ Laura and Marian went for a walk to the lake.
- **B** ☐ Sir Percival's lawyer came to Blackwater Park.
- **C** ☐ Marian went to meet the carriage that brought the post.
- **D** ☐ Laura told Marian about meeting Anne Catherick.
- **E** ☐ Sir Percival left Blackwater Park.
- **F** ☐ Count Fosco saw blood on the floor of the boat-house.
- **G** ☐ Sir Percival tried to make his wife sign a document.

Grammar

2 **Write the following sentences in reported speech. Use *tell* or *ask*.**

Laura to Marian: 'Have you written many letters recently?'
Laura asked Marian if she had written many letters recently.

1. Mr Merriman to Sir Percival: 'Don't worry.'
2. Laura to Marian: 'I know my husband has debts.'
3. Sir Percival to Lady Glyde: 'Sign the document.'
4. Laura to Marian: 'Shall I sign?'
5. Count Fosco to Marian: 'I've got good news for you.'
6. Marian to Laura: 'Did you hear or see anybody else?'
7. Count Fosco to Marian: 'There will be a change.'

Speaking

3 **Discuss the following about Chapter Three with a partner.**

1. The reason for signing the document.
2. The secret Anne Catherick and her mother know.
3. The meaning of *There will be a change tomorrow*.

PRE-READING ACTIVITY

Preliminary – Listening

▶ 7 **4 Listen to the start of Chapter Four and choose the correct answer, A, B or C.**

Laura decided to go to the boat-house at about
- ~~A~~ 2.30.
- B 2.15.
- C 2.45.

1 Sir Percival went out
- A before breakfast.
- B without having breakfast.
- C after breakfast.

2 The Count
- A went with Sir Percival.
- B stayed at home all morning.
- C had lunch alone.

3 Marian left the table
- A at the same time as Laura.
- B ten minutes before Laura.
- C ten minutes after Laura.

4 When Marian got to the boat-house,
- A she met Laura.
- B Laura wasn't there.
- C she played with the sand.

5 Marian found a piece of Laura's shawl
- A on a tree.
- B in the sand.
- C in the boat-house.

6 The path led to the
- A sea.
- B house.
- C lake.

7 When she got home, Marian met
- A Sir Percival.
- B Laura.
- C a servant.

39

Chapter 4

Danger at Blackwater Park

▶ 1   THE STORY CONTINUED BY MISS HALCOMBE.

19th June: The worst has come. Laura decided to go to the boat-house at about half past two. I said I would follow her soon after. Sir Percival went out immediately after breakfast. The Count passed the morning quietly in the house. Sir Percival didn't come back for lunch, but the Count had lunch with us. Laura left the table first, as planned. I waited ten minutes then left the Count and his wife still sitting at the table. It was now a quarter to three. When I got to the boat-house, Laura wasn't there. In the sand outside the boat-house there were large footprints* like a man's and smaller footprints which I was sure were Laura's. I followed the footprints along the sand, then through the trees. I found a piece of Laura's shawl on a tree. The path led to the back of the house. I was sure Laura had come back. I met one of the servants as I came into the house.

'Oh Miss Halcombe!' said the servant. 'Lady Glyde and Sir Percival are back, but I'm afraid something terrible has happened.'

'You don't mean an accident?' I asked.

'No, no, but Lady Glyde ran upstairs to her room in tears, and Sir Percival has said that Fanny must leave in an hour.'

Fanny was Laura's personal servant. She had brought her from Limmeridge and Laura was very fond of her. I went upstairs to Laura's room, but one of Sir Percival's servants was at her door.

footprint

'You can't come in,' she said. 'Sir Percival said so.'

I went downstairs to look for Sir Percival. I found him, the Count and Madame Fosco in the library, looking at a small piece of paper.

'Sir Percival!' I said angrily. 'Has Laura's room become a prison?'

'Yes,' he answered. 'Take care yours doesn't become a prison too!'

'I'll speak to my lawyer about this,' I shouted.

Instead of answering me, he looked at the Count. The Count said nothing. He looked at his wife and she came to my side and said:

'Sir Percival, I cannot stay in this house if you continue to behave in this terrible way with your wife and Miss Halcombe.'

Sir Percival looked at her in surprise. The Count took his wife's arm and said:

'I'm at your service, Eleanor, and at Miss Halcombe's too!'

'What do you mean?' cried Sir Percival.

'Madame Fosco's opinion is mine,' replied the Count.

Sir Percival left the room angrily.

I ran upstairs to Laura's room.

'How did you manage to get in?' she asked excitedly.

'The Count, of course,' I answered.

'Don't speak of him,' cried Laura. 'The Count is a miserable spy[*]!'

Before I could say anything, there was a knock at the door. It was Madame Fosco.

'Here's your handkerchief, Miss Halcombe. You left it downstairs.'

Her face was even whiter than usual. She looked past me to Laura. She had heard her. I thanked her and closed the door again.

'Oh Laura! She heard you call the Count a spy! We're in trouble now!'

---

spy a person who listens and watches in secret

'Well it's true,' said Laura. 'He was trying to listen to me and Anne Catherick yesterday in the boat-house. Then he told Sir Percival to watch for me and Anne all morning.'

'Did you see Anne?'

'No, when I got to the boat-house nobody was there. Then I looked about and there was a word written in the sand – LOOK – Under the sand I found a piece of paper signed by Anne.'

'Where is it?'

'Sir Percival has taken it from me!'

'Can you remember what it said?'

'Yes. She said she had seen a man there yesterday, so she couldn't come back today. She promised we'd meet again soon and that she'd tell me the Secret of my husband.'

'What about Sir Percival?'

'I had gone back into the boat-house to read the note again. Suddenly he was there. He said he'd already read the note and wanted to know what Anne had told me yesterday.'

'Did you tell him?'

'I had to Marian, he was hurting me. He thinks I know more. That's why he shut me in my room and he's decided to send Fanny away. Oh, Marian, what are we going to do?'

'Listen to me, my love, remember I'm here with you. I'm going to give Fanny two letters asking for help; one for our lawyer and one for your uncle. I need to go back downstairs now. They're probably talking about us. Here's the key. Lock the door and don't open it again until I come back.'

Before going downstairs, I locked the door of my own room and put the key in my pocket. As I went downstairs, I met Madame Fosco. She stopped me and said:

'I'm afraid I had to tell my husband what Lady Glyde said. He could see I was upset and I have no secrets from my husband.'

I felt cold inside as she said these words.

'Please excuse my sister. She spoke at a time when she was upset.'

'Don't worry, I forgive her,' said a voice behind me. It was the Count.

'You're very kind,' I replied.

I tried to continue but his eyes were watching me carefully. He kissed my hand and I wanted to scream, to shout, but I said nothing.

I ran back upstairs to my room to write the letters to my lawyer and Mr Fairlie. I wanted to give the letters to Fanny. It was a quarter to six. I had time to do everything before dinner. I walked quickly to the village and found Fanny. She was very upset about leaving Laura.

'Don't worry, Fanny,' I said. 'We'll look after you, but I need your help. Here are two letters. You must post this one when you get to London. This other one is for Mr Fairlie. Please give it to him yourself when you arrive at Limmeridge. These letters are very important Fanny.'

'I'll do anything to help you both,' said Fanny.

'Good. Now remember, don't miss the seven o'clock train tomorrow morning and good luck.'

When I got back to the house, Laura told me that Sir Percival had tried to enter her room but hadn't managed.

'He's mad, Marian,' said Laura. 'He hasn't found Anne Catherick and thinks I know more than I really do.'

'Don't worry, everything will be alright,' I said. Then I left her safely in her room to go down to dinner.

During dinner, nobody spoke much. After dinner, Count Fosco came and sat with his wife and me.

'Have you got any letters for the post, Miss Halcombe?' asked the Count, bringing the postbag to me.

'No, Count, thank you. No letters today.'

'I saw Madame Fosco looking at me. Then she drank her tea quickly and left the room. I tried to follow her but the Count stopped me and asked me for more tea. Then he started asking me questions about music. He continued talking, looking at me hard in the face and never waiting for an answer. He began to play the piano and sing loudly. He was very frightening. He only stopped when Sir Percival came into the room because of the noise. I took the opportunity to leave the room. Half an hour had passed since his wife had left us. I stayed with Laura till ten o'clock, then went downstairs to say goodnight. Sir Percival, the Count and his wife were sitting together. She had come back. But when? I said goodnight and went upstairs.

Back in my room, I went to the open window and looked out at the night. It was dark and quiet. Then suddenly, I saw Sir Percival and the Count in the garden below me. They couldn't see me. I heard the Count say:

'Come, let's go and talk in the library, Percival.'

I decided to climb out of my window and walk along the roof until I was above the library. I had to hear what they were saying. It had started to rain. The Count and Sir Percival were sitting near the open window under me. I could hear everything.

'Things have become serious, Percival,' said the Count. 'We must decide our future tonight. We both came back to this house from abroad with debts, didn't we?'

'Yes,' said Sir Percival. 'I needed a few thousand pounds and you a few hundred – and without the money we'd be in big trouble.'

'Yes, and so you married your wife. But what did I tell you about your wife and Miss Halcombe?'

'How should I know?' said Sir Percival.

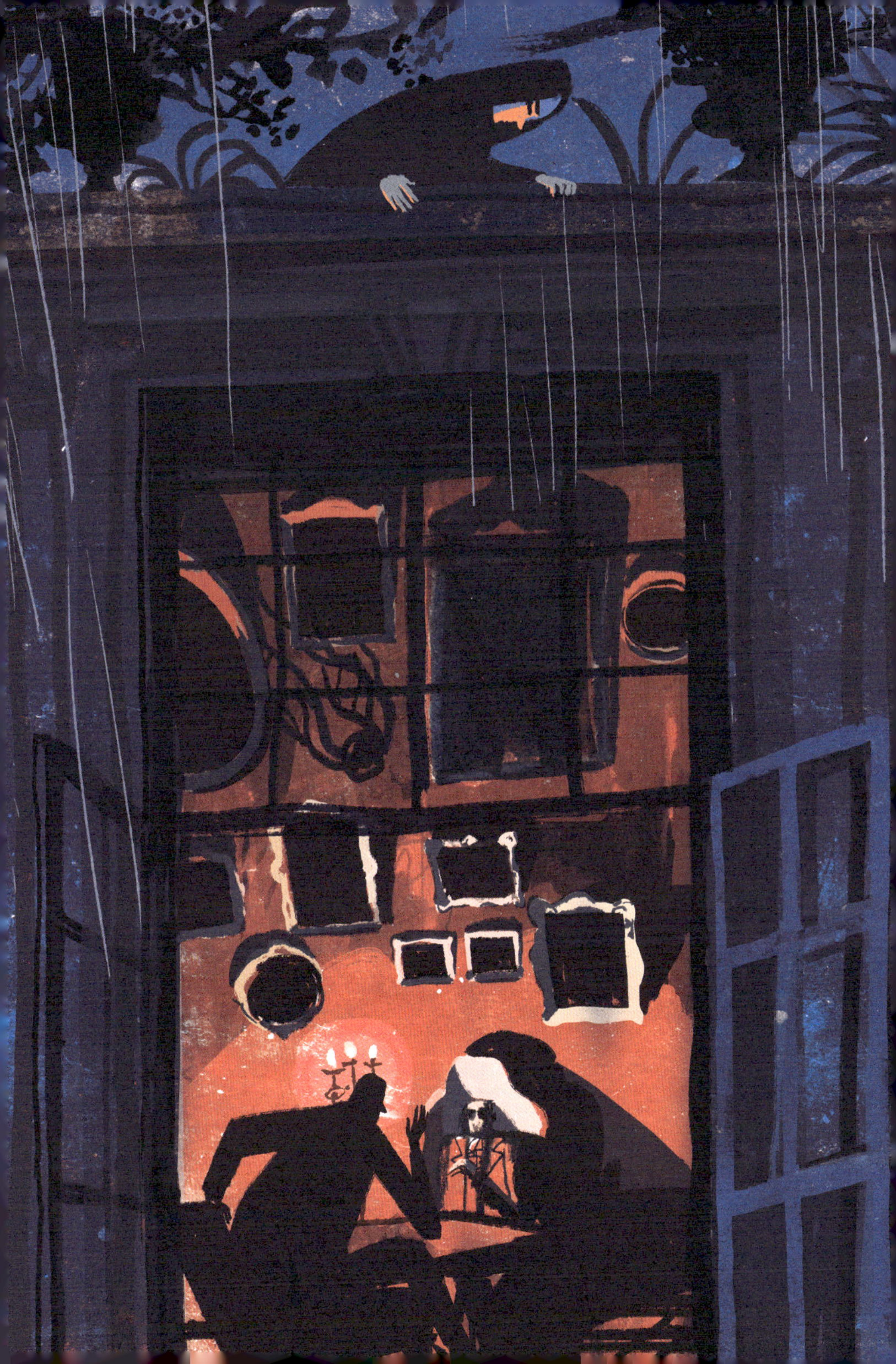

'I told you to keep calm. Instead, your anger* lost the signature on the document and so lost us the money. Then Miss Halcombe wrote to her lawyer for the first time and she's written to him again today.'

I couldn't believe it! How had he managed to read the letters when I had given them to Fanny?

'Thank your lucky stars,' continued the Count, 'that you have me in the house to solve all these problems as fast as you make them happen. You wanted to lock Miss Halcombe in her room! Are you mad? Can't you see she's a smart woman? She stands between us and your delicate pretty wife.'

'The money isn't the only problem,' said Sir Percival.

'We'll come to the second problem in a moment. You must leave everything in my hands from tonight. Do you agree Percival?'

'Yes, alright.'

'Right. First, how much of your wife's money have you got now?'

'Only £3000 – not enough to pay all my debts.'

'Is there nothing more you can get from your wife?'

'Nothing – unless she dies.'

It was now raining more heavily than before. There I was on the roof, wet and terrified.

'Well, Percival,' said the Count, 'and if Lady Glyde died, what would you get?'

'I'd get £20,000.'

'Well then; let me say your wife dies before the end of summer – '

'Drop it, Fosco!'

'You'd get £20,000.'

'And my wife's death would mean £10,000 in your wife's pocket.'

'Here is your position, Percival. If your wife lives, you pay your bills with her signature on the document. If your wife dies, you pay

anger what you feel when you are annoyed

them with her death! I have two months to find a solution. Now, Percival, the next problem is it Anne Catherick?'

'I've done my best to find Anne Catherick but without any success. Fosco! I'm a lost man if I don't find her!'

'Ha! Is it as serious as that?'

'More serious than the money problem. I showed you the note Anne Catherick hid in the sand for my wife, Fosco. She knows the Secret. Her mother told her.'

'So, even if I don't know this Secret,' said the Count, 'I can understand why you put her in the Asylum. So, Percival, what's the danger?'

'The danger is that Anne Catherick has spoken to Lady Glyde. My wife says she doesn't know the Secret but I don't believe her.'

'But doesn't she want to protect you as your wife?'

'No, because she's in love with another man, Hartright. He helped Anne Catherick at the start, and has spoken to her many times since then. So, he probably knows the Secret too. He's out of the country at the moment. He'd better stay there if he wants to stay alive.'

'How do you know?'

'Because some of my men watched him after he left Cumberland.'

'So, we must find Anne Catherick,' said the Count. 'What about her mother?'

'She won't tell the Secret. It'd be dangerous for her too.'

'One last question, Percival. What does Anne Catherick look like?'

'She looks like my wife after a bad illness.'

'What!!!' said the Count laughing. 'Well, well, well, I'll know Anne Catherick when I see her. That's enough for tonight. Sleep well Percival. You'll pay those bills and find Anne Catherick. I promise you.'

It was still raining. I felt cold inside and out, after everything I had heard.

AFTER-READING ACTIVITIES

Stop & Check

1 Answer the questions about Chapter 4.

Why did Sir Percival keep his wife in her room?
Because he wanted to find out if she really knew his secret or not.

1 What were Sir Percival, Count Fosco and his wife looking at when Laura went into the library?
2 Why was Madame Fosco angry with Lady Glyde?
3 Who told Sir Percival to go to the boat-house and wait for Anne Catherick and Laura?
4 Who did Marian decide to write to for help?
5 Who did Marian give the letters to?
6 Why didn't Marian follow Madame Fosco after dinner?
7 Why did Marian climb onto the roof?
8 What was the weather like that night?
9 How much money would Sir Percival get if his wife died?
10 How much money would Madame Fosco get after her niece's death?

Vocabulary

2 Read the definitions and complete the words from Chapter Four.

The first meal of the day.   b <u>r e a k f a s t</u>
1 Something you find near the sea.   s _ _ _
2 A small road.   p _ _ _
3 A place where you can find books.   l _ _ _ _ _ _
4 A place where you are kept if you do a crime.   p _ _ _ _ _
5 What you think.   o _ _ _ _ _ _
6 You use this to blow your nose.   h _ _ _ _ _ _ _ _ _ _
7 You use this to lock a door.   k _ _
8 You can hear this.   n _ _ _ _
9 The top of a house.   r _ _ _
10 You have to pay these.   b _ _ _ _

Preliminary Writing

3 You're Marian. Write a note to Frederick Fairlie. In your note you should

- explain what happened between Laura and Sir Percival
- ask him to let Laura go back to Limmeridge
- thank him for his help.

Write 35-45 words

Preliminary Speaking

4 Laura loves Limmeridge House. Now, talk to a partner about where you live and what you like and don't like about it.

PRE-READING ACTIVITY

Listening

5 Listen to the start of Chapter Five and decide if the sentences are true (T) or false (F).

		T	F
	Marian had a good night's sleep.	☐	✓
1	She doesn't feel well.	☐	☐
2	It's cold outside.	☐	☐
3	She'd rather sit at her desk than go to bed.	☐	☐
4	Count Fosco has just read a letter written by Marian.	☐	☐
5	Count Fosco thinks Marian is fantastic.	☐	☐
6	A doctor is looking after Marian and the Count wants to help him.	☐	☐
7	The Count has nothing to do.	☐	☐

Chapter 5

Illness and Lies

▶ 8   THE STORY CONTINUED BY MISS HALCOMBE.

20th June: Eight o'clock. I didn't sleep all night. I feel ill. My eyes are hot and I have a terrible headache. I can't write any more; I feel so cold and outside it's warm and sunny. I don't want to go to bed. I want to stay at my desk....'

Note by a true friend.
Miss Halcombe is ill and I've had the excellent opportunity to read this, her diary. She has such a good memory! What a wonderful woman! How clever she was to hear my conversation with Sir Percival. I'll try and help the doctor who's looking after her. I must go now. There's so much to do.
Fosco

THE STORY CONTINUED BY FREDERICK FAIRLIE
OF LIMMERIDGE HOUSE.

I have to write these lines, and remember dates. It's all very boring for me, but anyway, let me start.

At about the end of June, Fanny, my niece's servant, came to Limmeridge with a letter from Miss Halcombe. Fanny told me that when she left Blackwater Park, she went to stay the night in the village hotel. Between six o'clock and seven, Miss Halcombe came and gave her two letters. At nine o'clock, Madame Fosco came to see her with some messages from Miss Halcombe. Before telling her the messages, she offered to make Fanny a cup of tea. Very kind of my sister and not like her at all! After drinking the tea, Fanny fell asleep. When she woke up, Madame Fosco was gone. Fanny still had the letters but instead of being in her pocket, they were lying near her bed. In the morning, she left for London where she posted the first letter, and then she came here.

After Fanny had gone, I read Marian's letter. Why do people want to tell me about their problems? If I opened Limmeridge House to Lady Glyde, what would happen if Sir Percival followed her and got angry with me? I needed time to think so I wrote to dear Marian asking her to come and see me by herself. Then I received a letter from Gilmore's partner. He said he had received a letter from Miss Halcombe – the writing was hers on the envelope – but inside there was nothing. He was worried because he had written back to Miss Halcombe immediately but hadn't had any answer. Now he was annoying me with this problem! I wrote back to the lawyer and told him not to worry. Why worry? I wasn't worried. Marian hadn't written back to me either and she hadn't come to Limmeridge. Then, six days later, Count Fosco came to see me. He was so pleasant and understood perfectly how tired I was of all these letters. He told me that Marian was very ill. For some strange reason, she had been out in the rain. Then he told me it'd be better for Lady Glyde to come to Limmeridge as Marian had suggested. This might help bring peace between Laura and her husband. The Count promised that Sir Percival wouldn't follow his wife to Limmeridge. Before leaving, he said:

'Other people at Blackwater are looking after Miss Halcombe. Lady Glyde is useless in the sick-room. She's too upset about her sister's illness and is becoming ill herself. So, please tell Lady Glyde to come here now. Don't worry about the journey. I've taken a house in London. Lady Glyde can do the short journey from Blackwater Park to London. She can stay with her aunt and me for a few days, and then she can continue the journey to Limmeridge.'

So, I wrote the letter to Laura inviting her to Limmeridge. I knew she would say no – she wouldn't leave Blackwater Park while Marian was ill. I gave the letter to the Count and finally he went away.

I've said all that I have to say. I did everything for the best so I hope nobody will blame me for what happened later. I'm so tired and heartbroken. Need I say more?

THE STORY CONTINUED BY ELIZA MICHELSON – HEAD OF THE SERVANTS AT BLACKWATER PARK.

I'm asked to speak about Miss Halcombe's illness and about what made Lady Glyde leave Blackwater Park for London.

Miss Halcombe's serious illness began about mid-June. I found her in her room with a burning temperature and she was very confused*. Lady Glyde was too upset to help but the Count and his wife were very kind. Sir Percival sent for the doctor, Mr Dawson. The Count tried to give the doctor some advice but the doctor got angry with him, so the Count went for a walk to the boat-house. He didn't come back till seven o'clock that evening. The next day, Miss Halcombe was worse. I heard the Count tell Sir Percival that he was going to the lake again to study. The Count was such a kind man and was always

---

confused when you can't think clearly

interested in everybody. I remember when Fanny had to go; he was worried about her and asked me where she was going and how she would travel. On the third day, Miss Halcombe was even worse. As I came downstairs that afternoon, the Count came back from his walk. I heard Sir Percival ask him:

'Have you found her?'

The Count said nothing, but smiled. Before following Sir Percival into the library, the Count spoke to me.

'You seem very tired, Mrs Michelson. You need some help. Madame Fosco must travel to London, either tomorrow or the day after, just for the day and she'll bring back a good nurse to help you.'

The night passed as usual, but there was no change in Miss Halcombe. The next day, Madame Fosco left for London and Miss Halcombe seemed a bit better. Lady Glyde stayed beside her sister's bed all the time. Madame Fosco came back that night with the new nurse, Mrs Rubelle. She was a foreigner. She wore rather expensive clothes and was very quiet. Lady Glyde didn't like her and neither did Mr Dawson. He told me to watch her. However, I never saw anything strange and Mrs Rubelle was a good nurse.

Count Fosco went to London for a week. Before leaving, he told Lady Glyde to wait another few days but if there was no change in Miss Halcombe, she should call a doctor from London.

Sir Percival began to drink more and eat less. Maybe he was missing his friend, Count Fosco and was worried about Lady Glyde who became more tired and weaker every day. In the next few days, Miss Halcombe seemed to be a bit better, but then on the third day after the Count had left, she suddenly got worse. When Mr Dawson saw Miss Halcombe, he too was worried. Next morning, he sent for a doctor from London. Count Fosco came back and immediately went to see Miss Halcombe.

'It's Typhus Fever*,' he said. 'Mr Dawson, I'll blame you if this unhappy lady dies!'

The doctor from London came at about six o'clock. He confirmed it was Typhus Fever. Five days passed. Madame Fosco, Mrs Rubelle and I looked after Miss Halcombe. She was now very, very ill. Lady Glyde came to see her sister two or three times a day. On the tenth day, the doctor from London said Miss Halcombe was no longer in danger. During this time, Count Fosco had gone to London again for the day. All Miss Halcombe needed now was rest and care. Lady Glyde had been so strong till now, but on hearing the good news, all her energy suddenly left her. She was so weak that she had to stay in bed. Count Fosco argued with Mr Dawson and the doctor left Blackwater Park and never came back.

Sir Percival called for me. I was very upset when he told me to send all the servants away. He wanted to close the house by the end of the month to save money. They all went away the next day.

A few days later, Sir Percival spoke to me in the library. Count Fosco was there too. He told me that Mr Fairlie had invited Lady Glyde and her sister to pass the autumn at Limmeridge House, but first I had to go and look for a nice place in Torquay where the ladies could stay and enjoy some warm weather before going to Limmeridge House. So, I left for Torquay the next day but I didn't find anything there for the money Sir Percival wanted to spend.

When I came back, there had been another change. Count Fosco and his wife had left Blackwater Park for their new house in London. I went to see Lady Glyde. She hadn't left her room for days. She was much better even if she was still weak and nervous. She was worried because that morning she hadn't heard any news about Miss Halcombe. We decided to go together to Miss Halcombe's room to see her. As we came out of Lady Glyde's room, we met Sir Percival.

Typhus Fever a very serious illness

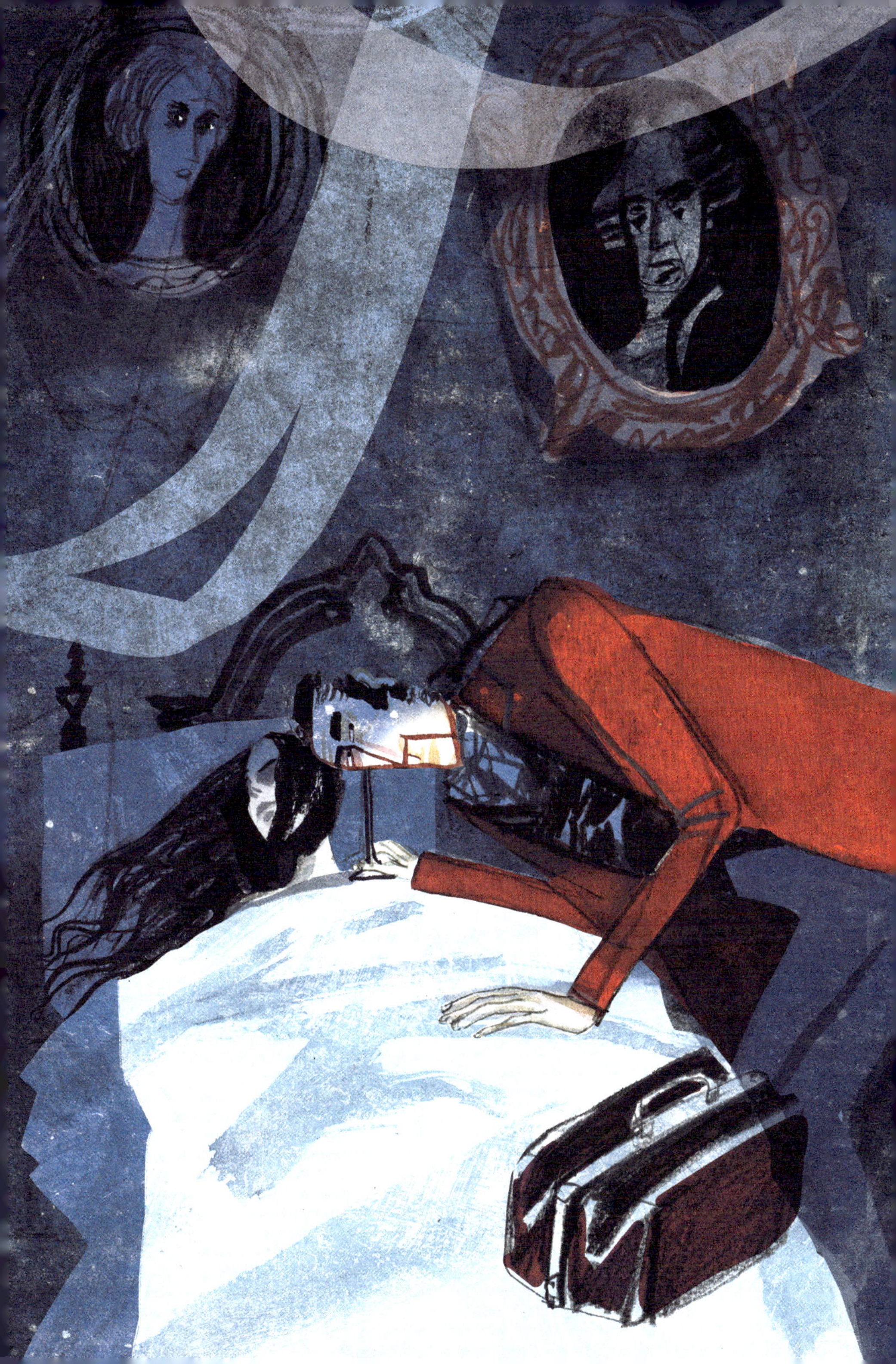

'Where are you going?' he said to Lady Glyde.

'To Marian's room,' she answered.

'You'll not find her there,' said Sir Percival. 'She left the house yesterday morning with Fosco and his wife.'

'Impossible!' cried Lady Glyde. She ran to Miss Halcombe's room and opened the door. He was right – Marian had gone!

'Please, tell me what all this means Sir Percival,' said Lady Glyde.

'It means,' he answered, 'that Miss Halcombe was strong enough yesterday morning to go with Fosco to London on her way to Limmeridge. Don't worry; she has Fosco, his wife and Mrs Rubelle who will look after her.'

'Why is Marian going to Limmeridge without me?' said Lady Glyde.

'Because your uncle won't receive you till he has seen your sister first,' replied Sir Percival. 'Don't you remember reading the letter he wrote to her at the start of her illness?'

'Yes, I remember,' said Lady Glyde. 'But why did she leave without saying goodbye?'

'Because she knew you'd try to stop her,' said Sir Percival. He turned and went downstairs.

'Mrs Michelson,' said Lady Glyde, 'I must follow Marian! Please, come downstairs with me to speak to Sir Percival.'

Sir Percival was sitting at the table drinking.

'Please let me follow Marian at once by the afternoon train,' Lady Glyde said to her husband.

'You must wait till tomorrow,' replied Sir Percival. 'I'll write to Fosco tonight to tell him to meet you at the station when you get to London. Then he'll take you to sleep at your aunt's for the night.'

'I'd rather not stay in London to sleep.'

'You must. You can't do the whole journey to Cumberland in one day. You must rest a night in London,' he said angrily. Then he stood up and went out to the garden.

The next day, I went with Lady Glyde to the station and waited with her until she left on the train for London. Later that same day, I went for a walk in the garden and who did I see? Mrs Rubelle!

'I thought you were in London,' I said to her.

'Certainly not!' she said. 'I've never left Blackwater Park and neither has Miss Halcombe!'

I was too surprised to say anything. Then Sir Percival arrived.

'You can't believe it, can you?' he said laughing. 'Here! Come and see for yourself.'

He led me to the other side of the house and pointed to a window on the first floor.

'Miss Halcombe is in there,' he said.

'Sir Percival – I wish to leave Blackwater Park!' I said.

'Go if you want,' he said, 'but remember, this was the only way to make my wife leave. She really needed a change of air, but she didn't want to leave Marian. I lied to her for her own good.'

I didn't believe him but I said nothing.

'I'm leaving this house forever tomorrow morning,' he said. 'Mrs Rubelle is going to London tonight. If you leave, Miss Halcombe will be all alone.'

'I'll stay then,' I said.

That night, Sir Percival left Blackwater Park. I don't know if he was excited or angry but he was very strange. I still don't know where he is now. This is the end of my part of this sad family story.

AFTER-READING ACTIVITIES

Stop & Check

1 **Decide if the following sentences about Chapter Five are true (T) or false (F).**

	T	F
Mr Frederick Fairlie was happy to write his part of the story.	☐	✓
1 Madame Fosco seemed unusually kind to Fanny.	☐	☐
2 When Fanny woke up, the letters were in a different place.	☐	☐
3 The lawyer was worried because he couldn't understand Marian's writing.	☐	☐
4 The Count said Lady Glyde should travel to Limmeridge without breaking her journey.	☐	☐
5 Mrs Michelson thought Count Fosco was a nice man.	☐	☐
6 The doctor from London agreed with the Count about Marian's illness.	☐	☐
7 Sir Percival told Lady Glyde she could leave for Limmeridge immediately.	☐	☐

Speaking

2 **Sir Percival lied to his wife and Mrs Michelson when he said that Marian had left Blackwater Park for London. Discuss the following with a partner.**

- Why do you think Sir Percival lied?
- Why do people sometimes tell lies?

Vocabulary

3 Circle the correct word to complete the sentences.

During/*While* her illness, Marian had a very high temperature.
1 *If/Although* Mrs Michelson didn't really like Mrs Rubelle, she couldn't complain about her as a nurse.
2 Mr Dawson didn't like Mrs Rubelle and Laura didn't like her *else/either*.
3 Sir Percival wanted to save money, *however/therefore* he sent his servants away.
4 Madame Fosco looked after Marian. *Actually/Meanwhile*, the Count helped Sir Percival.
5 Sir Percival *extremely/definitely* got angry easily.

PRE-READING ACTIVITY

Listening

▶ 9 **4 Listen to the start of Chapter Six and circle the correct word(s) to make true sentences.**

Hester Pinhorn was Count Fosco's *cook*/*doctor*.
1 Hester worked for Count Fosco last *spring/summer*.
2 Hester had been at Count Fosco's house for a *long/short* time when Lady Glyde arrived.
3 The doctor said there was something wrong with Lady Glyde's *heart/head*.
4 Lady Glyde died on *25th July/26th July*.
5 Lady Glyde's husband was in *Cumberland/abroad*.
6 *Madame/Count* Fosco arranged to take the body back to Cumberland.
7 Lady Glyde's *mother/father* was already buried in Cumberland.

Chapter 6

A Death in London

▶ 9   THE STORY CONTINUED BY COUNT FOSCO'S COOK
IN LONDON, HESTER PINHORN.

Last summer, I worked for Count Fosco and his wife. Just after I had started, Madame Fosco's niece, Lady Glyde, came to stay with them. She was ill and they told me to cook nice things for her. In fact, that afternoon, Lady Glyde became very ill. The doctor came and said there was something seriously wrong with her heart. She died two days later. It was 25th July. I remember because the doctor came and wrote it down on the death certificate*. Count Fosco was terribly upset when he heard the news. Poor man, he was usually so full of fun, much nicer than his wife. We were told that the dead lady's husband was abroad, so Madame Fosco made all the arrangements to take the body back to Cumberland where the dead lady's mother was already buried.

▶ 10   To answer the last question: I never saw Count Fosco give any medicine to Lady Glyde. As far as I know, he was never alone with Lady Glyde; only his wife stayed up to look after the poor girl during the night.

WALTER HARTRIGHT'S STORY.

I arrived in London after my adventures in Central America in

certificate official document confirming true information

October 1850. Laura Fairlie was still in my thoughts. I went to see my mother and sister. As soon as I saw my mother, I knew she had sad news for me. Laura was dead! The only thing I could do now was to go and visit her grave*. I left for Cumberland and arrived in the afternoon. I walked along those familiar paths, and on my way, I passed Limmeridge House. I remembered Laura in the garden laughing as I taught her how to draw. I reached the church where I had met the woman in white and where Laura was now buried beside her mother. I found the grave and stayed there for a long time just looking at her name on the stone. Oh my love! My love! Then I heard a noise. I looked up and saw two women coming towards me. They came nearer. They were looking at me but I couldn't see their faces very well.

Then they stopped and one of the women pushed back her hood*. It was Marian Halcombe. She seemed older and frightened. Then the other woman came towards me. We stood face to face. She pushed back her hood too – it was Laura, Lady Glyde.

A week has passed since that extraordinary meeting. All three of us are now in London. We're living in two small rooms in a poor part of the city. I draw for some magazines to earn some money for me and the ladies (I've told everybody they're my sisters). We're hiding in London. Only Marian and I know Laura is still alive. Her husband and her aunt now have Laura's money. Marian and I will have to fight to give Laura back her life. Laura has changed; from her face, you can see that she has suffered so much, and she still can't think clearly. All she says is:

'They've tried to make me forget everything, Walter; but I remember Marian and I remember you.'

Now I must tell the story of Laura and Marian.

grave where the dead are buried   **hood** part of a coat to cover the head

Shortly after Lady Glyde left Blackwater Park, a letter arrived from Count Fosco's wife to say Laura was dead. Three weeks passed before Marian felt strong enough to go to London to see her lawyer. She wanted to find out more about how Lady Glyde had died. Count Fosco received the lawyer well and let him talk to the doctor and the servants who had been in the house at that time. The lawyer saw nothing strange in Lady Glyde's death and thought that Miss Halcombe was imagining things that didn't exist.

Meanwhile Miss Halcombe had returned to Limmeridge House to get any information she could. Mr Fairlie had received a letter from his sister, Madame Fosco, telling him of his niece's death. He agreed to bury her beside her mother. Count Fosco had come to Limmeridge for the funeral* on 30th July. Count Fosco had stayed at Limmeridge House for two days and had written a letter to Mr Fairlie who had been too tired to receive him. In the letter Count Fosco said that they had found Anne Catherick near Blackwater Park and that she was now back in the Asylum. He said Anne Catherick was now absolutely mad and kept telling all the doctors and nurses that she was Lady Glyde. He told Mr Fairlie to be careful if he ever received a letter from this mad woman. Miss Halcombe read the letter when she arrived at Limmeridge. They also gave her the clothes Lady Glyde had worn at her aunt's house. Madame Fosco had sent them to Cumberland.

It was now early September and Miss Halcombe became ill again. After a month, she felt a bit better. During this time, she had had no news about Sir Percival, but she had received letters from Madame Fosco asking her how she was. Miss Halcombe didn't answer them, but she paid a man to watch Count Fosco's house in London: she discovered nothing. As for Sir Percival, he was now in Paris with some friends.

funeral when you bury a dead person

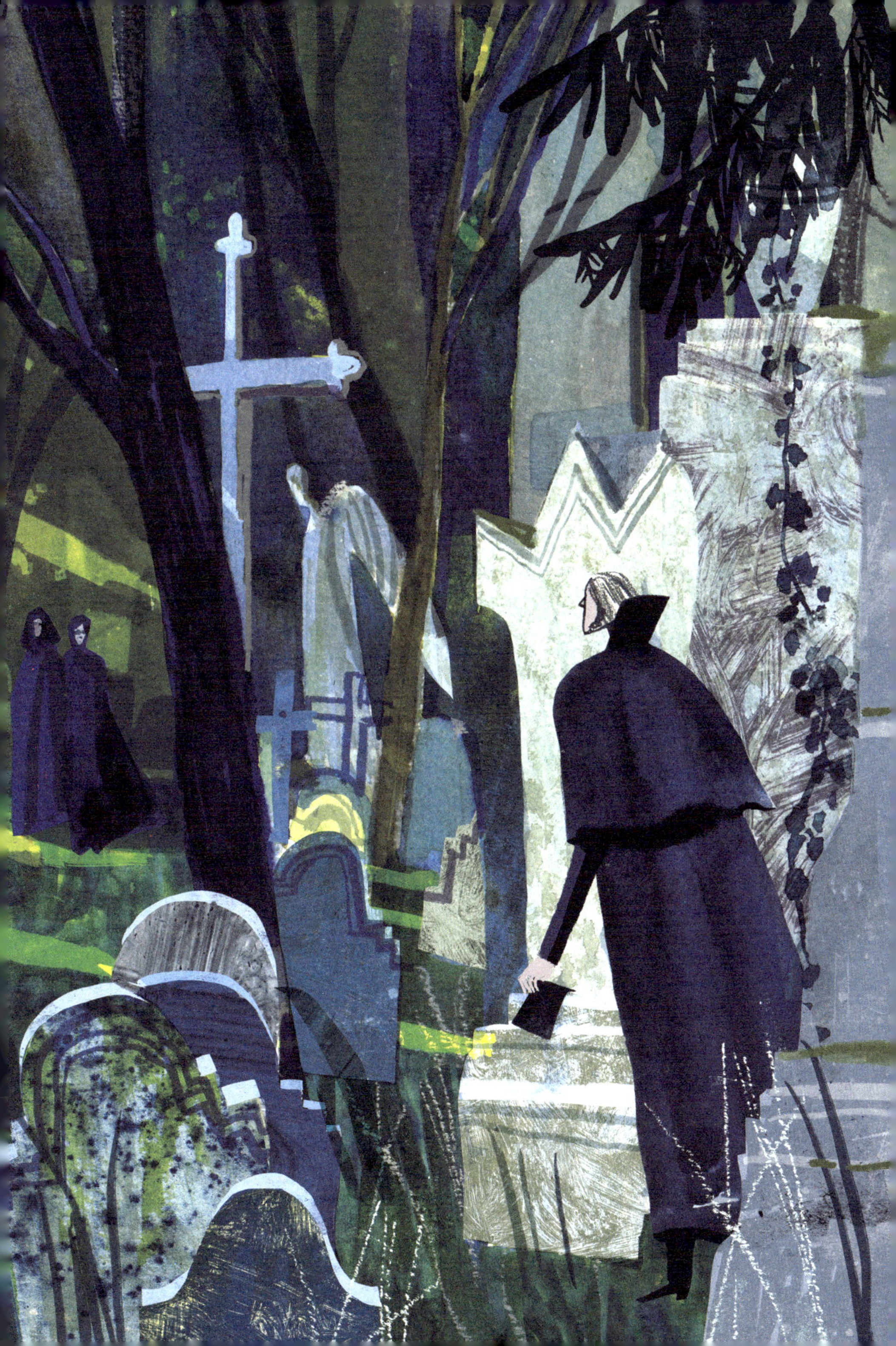

Then Miss Halcombe decided to visit the Asylum in London where Fosco said Anne Catherick was. It was now October. The owner of the Asylum told her that Count Fosco had brought Anne Catherick back on 27th July. A nurse took Miss Halcombe to the garden where Anne Catherick was walking. As soon as Anne Catherick saw Miss Halcombe, she ran into her arms. In that moment, Miss Halcombe recognised her sister. The nurse let them speak alone for a moment and Miss Halcombe told Lady Glyde that she would help her escape from the Asylum. Then, Miss Halcombe went to speak to the nurse, gave her some money and asked her to meet her the next day at 3 o'clock outside the Asylum. The nurse was a young girl who was getting married soon and wanted to start a business with her husband. Miss Halcombe offered her £400 if she would help her patient to escape from the Asylum and the girl said yes. The following morning, the nurse brought Lady Glyde to Miss Halcombe who was waiting just outside the walls of the Asylum. Miss Halcombe took her sister back to London, caught the first train for Cumberland and arrived at Limmeridge House that night. During the journey, Lady Glyde tried to tell her sister what had happened even if she was weak and confused. This is her story:

Lady Glyde couldn't remember the exact date she arrived in London. Count Fosco was waiting for her at the station. He said he would take her to see Miss Halcombe who hadn't left for Cumberland yet because she still wasn't strong enough. He took her to a house in a small street (not his house but she didn't know that) and told her to wait in the living room. Count Fosco came back with two men who asked Lady Glyde many strange questions. Then Count Fosco came back with a glass of water for Lady Glyde and after drinking it, she fell asleep. From this point, she couldn't remember anything very well. She didn't know how much time had passed but when she woke up, she was in the Asylum, and everybody was calling her Anne Catherick. She then realised that the clothes she was wearing all had Anne Catherick's name on them. That was all she could remember. She had been in the Asylum from 27th July to 15th October, when Miss Halcombe came for her.

They arrived at Limmeridge late on the evening of the 15th. Next morning, Miss Halcombe went to see Mr Fairlie to tell him what had happened. Mr Fairlie didn't believe her even after she brought Lady Glyde to his room. He remembered Count Fosco's letter and was sure this woman was the mad woman, Anne Catherick. Even the servants in the house weren't sure it was Lady Glyde – she used to be so pretty – now she seemed much older and thinner, and her mind was confused. Nobody believed this poor young woman was really Lady Glyde.

It was now too dangerous to stay at Limmeridge so Miss Halcombe decided to take her sister back to London. As they left Limmeridge House, Lady Glyde asked to see her mother's grave for what might be the last time. This is when the future of our three lives started again.

This was the story of the past – the story so far as we knew it then.

It was obvious Count Fosco had taken Anne Catherick to his house, telling everybody that she was Lady Glyde. It was also now clear to me that Lady Glyde had taken the dead Anne Catherick's place in the Asylum. This was the horrible crime Count Fosco and Sir Percival had planned so well, to get their hands on Laura's money. They were dangerous and Marian and I had to protect Laura from them.

Nobody bothered us in our little house in London and Laura and Marian never went out without me. I worked and Marian kept the house clean and we both looked after Laura. After all that had happened to her, poor Laura seemed even more like Anne Catherick than before. She still couldn't remember very much but we tried to help her by speaking every day about the happy times at Limmeridge, when I first went there and taught her to draw. I began to teach her to draw again and this slowly helped her mind.

I decided to go and see Miss Halcombe's lawyer with all the information I had, to see what our position was. I had forgotten that Sir Percival was probably back in London now and that his men might be outside the lawyer's office, ready to follow me home.

I told Mr Kyrle, Mr Gilmore's partner, everything I knew. He told me we had nothing to show that the person who had died wasn't Lady Glyde. The only thing that could help our situation was if we could find out the exact date when Lady Glyde had travelled from Limmeridge to London. If this was after the date on the death certificate, then this would definitely show that the dead woman wasn't Lady Glyde. He gave me a letter for Miss Halcombe and as I was leaving, I asked him:

'Do you know if Sir Percival Glyde is still in Paris?'

'He has returned to London,' replied the lawyer. 'His lawyers told me yesterday.'

I went out and started walking along the street. I looked back – two men were following me. Fortunately, there was a carriage nearby. I jumped in and managed to get away from them. When I got home, it was dark. I told Marian all my news and I gave her the letter Mr Kyrle had given me for her. It was from Count Fosco. It said:

Don't be afraid! Do nothing more than you have already done. She has found a new asylum in your heart and I'll leave her there if you do no more.

Please don't put me in the position where I have to take further action. If Mr Hartright returns to England, don't contact him.

F

'He's trying to frighten you,' I said. 'This means he must be frightened himself.'

Marian said nothing but I could see the anger in her eyes.

The next day, I went to Blackwater. I wanted to discover the exact date Laura had left Blackwater Park to see if it was after the date on the death certificate. Nobody knew the exact date. What next? If we knew Sir Percival's Secret, we could make him tell us the date. I went into the village and found out that after I had seen Anne Catherick at Mrs Fairlie's grave, she had gone to London with her friend Mrs Clements. I decided to go back to London to speak to this woman.

AFTER-READING ACTIVITIES

Stop & Check

1 **Read the questions about Chapter Six and choose the correct answer, A, B, or C.**

When did the cook say Lady Glyde had died?
- ~~A~~ Two days after arriving at the Count's house.
- **B** The same afternoon she arrived at the Count's house.
- **C** The night after arriving at the Count's house.

1 How did Walter Hartright find out about Laura's death?
- **A** He read about it in a newspaper.
- **B** Marian wrote to him.
- **C** His mother told him.

2 Where did Walter Hartright meet Marian and Laura again?
- **A** At Limmeridge House.
- **B** At Mrs Fairlie's grave.
- **C** In London.

3 Who wrote to Marian about Laura's death?
- **A** Madame Fosco.
- **B** Mr Fairlie.
- **C** Count Fosco.

4 What did the Count tell Mr Fairlie?
- **A** Anne Catherick was still near Blackwater Park.
- **B** Anne Catherick thought she was Lady Glyde.
- **C** He had a letter for him from Anne Catherick.

5 Where had Sir Percival gone?
- **A** To Blackwater Park.
- **B** To London.
- **C** To Paris.

6 Who helped Lady Glyde escape from the Asylum?
- **A** Walter Hartright.
- **B** Marian Halcombe.
- **C** Mr Fairlie.

7 Who had written the letter Mr Kyrle had for Miss Halcombe?
- **A** Mr Gilmore.
- **B** Sir Percival.
- **C** Count Fosco.

Grammar

2 Circle the correct word(s) to make true sentences about the story.

Walter Hartright *couldn't*/*shouldn't* believe it when he saw Laura was alive.

1 Marian and Laura *don't have to*/*mustn't* go out alone in London because it's dangerous.
2 Now Marian and Walter *can*/*need* to fight to give Laura back her life.
3 The Count agreed that Lady Glyde *should*/*ought* be buried beside her mother.
4 The Count told Mr Fairlie that Anne Catherick *might*/*must* write to him in the future.
5 Laura *will*/*needn't* worry any more because Marian and Walter are with her now.

PRE-READING ACTIVITY

Listening

▶ 11 **3 Listen to the start of Chapter Seven and answer the questions.**

Did Mrs Clements know about Anne Catherick's death?
No, she didn't.
1 Did Anne feel alright in Grimsby?
2 Was the village of Sandon near Blackwater Park?
3 Did Anne go to Blackwater Lake on foot?
4 Did Count Fosco speak to Mrs Clements at the lake?
5 Was Anne awake when Count Fosco came to see her?
6 In the Count's opinion, would Anne be well enough to travel after three days?
7 Were Anne and Mrs Clements going to go to London by train?

Chapter 7

A Family Secret

▶ 11 Mrs Clements was obviously very fond of Anne Catherick. I couldn't say anything about Anne's death yet, but I told her I'd contact her if I had any news. This is what she told me:

'I stayed with Anne Catherick in London, then we went to Grimbsy. Poor Anne wasn't well. The doctor said she had a heart problem. When she felt better, Anne decided to go back to Hampshire to speak to Lady Glyde. We stayed in a village called Sandon, quite far from Blackwater Park. Anne walked there and back every time she went to speak to Lady Glyde. Then Anne became ill again. I went to the lake to tell Lady Glyde that Anne couldn't come, but instead I met Count Fosco. He said he had a message from Lady Glyde; she said that we had to go back to London immediately before Sir Percival discovered us. I told the Count that Anne was too ill to travel and he kindly offered to come and see her. He had studied medicine. When he saw Anne, she was sleeping. However, he left some medicine for her and told me she'd be fit to travel in three days. He said he'd meet us at Blackwater Station to put us on the train to London. He also said that Lady Glyde was planning to go to London a few days after us so Anne could meet her there.

The Count was right; three days later, Anne was better. Before leaving, the Count told me to send my address in London to Lady Glyde. Two weeks later, a lady came with a message from Lady Glyde. She asked me to go with her because Lady Glyde wanted to arrange a meeting with Anne. I left Anne at home and went with the lady. Then a strange thing happened; we were walking along the street when suddenly I turned round and the lady had gone. I waited half an hour, but she still hadn't come back so I went home. When I got home, Anne was gone. I went to the Asylum the next day but she wasn't there. Then, I wrote to Mrs Catherick but she hadn't seen Anne either; I still don't know where she is.'

I then asked her about Mrs Catherick.

'We used to live near each other in Old Welmingham – there is only the old church left – everybody now lives in the new town called Welmingham. Mr Catherick looked after the vestry* and Mrs Catherick had been a servant to a family that lived at Varneck Hall, near Southampton. Mr Catherick was in love with her but Mrs Catherick wasn't a good wife. Four months after they were married, the whole village was talking about her.

'Why, what happened?' I asked.

'It was about Sir Percival and Mrs Catherick. Sir Percival came to the village in April 1827 and Anne was born in June. One night, Mr Catherick was very upset. He had found expensive gifts in his wife's bag and he had seen his wife talking and laughing with Sir Percival Glyde outside the vestry. The next day, Mr Catherick left the village forever. Sir Percival left the next evening, but Mrs Catherick stayed in the village. She said it was all a big mistake. She lived well enough – everybody in the village said Sir Percival sent her money.'

'Mrs Clements,' I said, 'do you know why Sir Percival Glyde put Anne in the Asylum?'

'Anne told me that her mother knew a secret about Sir Percival. One evening, Mrs Catherick told Anne about it and when Sir Percival found out, he put Anne in the Asylum.'

vestry room next to a church to keep things in

Before leaving, Mrs Clements gave me Mrs Catherick's address in Welmingham. Three days later, I knocked on Mrs Catherick's door.

'Mrs Catherick,' I said, 'I've come to speak to you about your daughter.'

'Have you come to tell me she's dead?' said Mrs Catherick.

'Yes,' I replied.

'No other reason?' she asked coldly.

'Yes, I'm interested in Sir Percival Glyde and what happened at Old Welmingham before your daughter was born.'

Her face became red for a moment.

'Destroy him for yourself,' she said.

'You're afraid of Sir Percival Glyde,' I said. 'He comes from a great family – '

She laughed and said: 'Yes, a great family – especially on his mother's side. You know nothing of Sir Percival.'

'I'll tell you what I don't think,' I said. 'I don't think Sir Percival is Anne's father.'

'Go!' she shouted angrily.

'There was no love between you and Sir Percival when your husband saw you speaking together at the church vestry.'

This time her face became white. Those last words had frightened her.

'Go!' she said – 'and never come back!'

I left the room.

The next day, I decided to go to the vestry of Old Welmingham church. Mrs Catherick had been so frightened when I spoke of this place, I was sure I'd find the answer to Sir Percival's Secret there. Nobody knew much about Sir Percival's family. Maybe there was a register* in the vestry with details of his parents' marriage.

---

register a book with dates of marriages etc.

The vestry was next to the church. I met the man who now looked after the vestry and he took me there. He had problems opening the door – it was old and heavy but finally he managed. It was quite a big room and it was full of things belonging to the church. I asked to see the marriage register. The man looked about and finally found it under lots of other papers.

'Shouldn't you keep it in a safer place?' I asked the man.

'That's what my old boss, Mr Wansborough, always used to say,' said the man. 'Mr Wansborough was the vestry lawyer and looked after any church business. He used to keep a copy of the register in his office at Knowlesbury. His son is now the vestry lawyer and works from his father's old office.'

I found the marriage certificate of Sir Percival's parents written at the bottom of a page. There was nothing strange about it except that it was written in a much smaller space than the other marriages on the same page. There was still nothing about the Secret.

I decided to go to Knowlesbury to speak to the vestry lawyer. Mr Wansborough was very pleasant and showed me the copy of the register his father had kept. I opened the book at the page I had seen in the original register in the vestry. This time there was nothing at the bottom of the page, just a space. All the other marriages were there except the marriage of Sir Percival's parents. It was obvious that Sir Percival had written it in the other book; it was false. I had never thought that Sir Percival was an imposter*: not from a rich family, not a 'Sir', not the true owner of Blackwater Park. This was his Secret! If anybody found out, he'd lose everything. I decided to go back to the vestry to get the page from the register. I thanked the lawyer and left.

imposter a person who makes everybody think he/she is somebody else

It was getting dark. I ran as fast as I could. Near the church, I met the man I had spoken to that morning. He told me that somebody had stolen the keys of the vestry from his house. He got a light and we both went to the vestry. We turned the corner to the church and – I couldn't believe it – the vestry was on fire! There were already flames* coming out of the roof! I ran to the door. Somebody was behind it trying to get out but couldn't get the door open. "Help" I heard. I recognised the voice – it was Sir Percival. I tried to break the door down but it was too heavy. I climbed up onto the roof and broke the window, but the room was full of flames and smoke. There was nothing I could do to save Sir Percival.

Now that I knew he was dead, I felt exhausted*. I sat down on the ground and waited for the firemen to arrive. They found Sir Percival, face down, behind the door.

The next day I wrote to Marian to tell her what had happened. I felt sad and weak. The register was lost in the fire with Sir Percival. Marian's reply arrived telling me that they were well – the only bright moment in my day. Later that day, I received a letter from Mrs Catherick:

Sir,

You didn't come back to tell me, but I know the news. Thank you Sir, I've waited for this moment for twenty-three years. I'm old now, so I want to tell you some things about my private life. In 1827, I was a beautiful young woman, married to a fool for a husband. I also knew a rich man. I won't call him by his name. Why should I? It wasn't his own. He never had a name: you know that now, don't you? I liked pretty things and he gave me presents. He asked me for the key of the vestry and I got it for him. He didn't tell me why he needed the key so I watched him and I found out. I didn't really care that he'd written something in the register. I knew it was wrong to add

flame

exhausted very tired

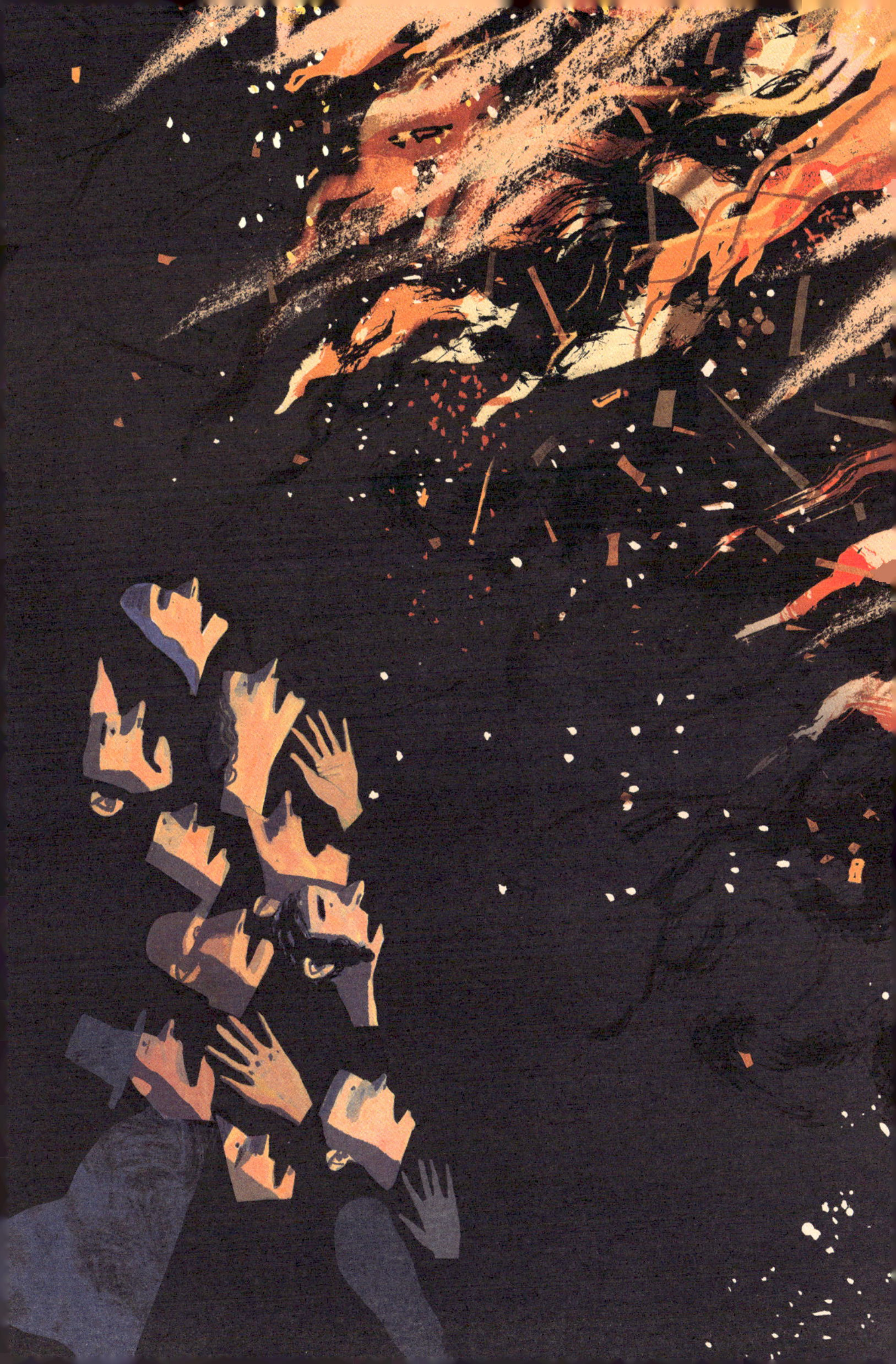

a marriage to the register, but I didn't know it was a crime – and he had promised me a gold watch. I told him that if he told me his story, I wouldn't say anything about it to anybody.

After his parents died, he came to England and went to stay in Blackwater Park, saying that he was the owner. Nobody knew anything about him because his mother and father had always lived a quiet life. The only problem was that, if he wanted to borrow money on the property, he needed his birth certificate and his parents' marriage certificate. His birth certificate wasn't a problem because he was born abroad, but the marriage certificate was a problem, and that's why he came to Old Welmingham. His father, Sir Felix hadn't married his mother because she was already a married woman. She had married a bad man in Ireland who had left her for another woman. Sir Percival wrote the false marriage note in the register. Then my husband saw us together and thought we were lovers. I asked him to tell my husband the truth but he said no, because if my husband and the village people were busy talking about me, then nobody would notice his crime. I said I'd tell everybody, but he said I had helped him so I'd go to prison too. I was frightened and that's when I started to hate him. He said that he'd send me money, but that I must never tell anybody. He also told me to stay in Welmingham so he knew where I was all the time. I had no friends here, so nobody to talk to.

As for my daughter, she was always a worry to me from first to last, always weak in the head. Sometimes Sir Percival let me leave this place for short trips. One time, I went to Limmeridge because my sister was dying. I thought I'd get some money from her when she died but she had nothing. Anne came with me and went to school there. The teacher, Mrs Fairlie, who had married one of the most handsome men in England, liked Anne a lot. Anne spent a lot of time at Limmeridge House where they gave her the stupid idea that she should wear white.

Years passed, people forgot, so things got easier for me. One morning, I received a letter from that highly born man (now dead). I had asked to go away for a few days but he said no. I was so angry with him that day that I told Anne that he had a Secret and that if I told everybody, I would destroy him. I said no more. I realised I had made a mistake. Anne had been particularly crazy that year and I was afraid she might repeat my words in the town. The next day, he came to my house. When he saw my daughter in the room, he told her to leave. Anne didn't like him and said: 'I'll tell your Secret; I can destroy you.' This is why he put Anne in the Asylum. I told him again and again that she had only repeated my words and that she didn't really know the Secret but he wouldn't listen.

Poor Anne! After reading the letter, there was still one question in my mind: who was Anne Catherick's father?

AFTER-READING ACTIVITIES

Stop & Check

1 **Answer the questions about Chapter Seven.**

Why was Anne fit to travel to London after three days?
Because she took the medicine the Count left her.
1 Why did Mrs Clements leave Anne on her own?
2 How did Mrs Clements know Mrs Catherick?
3 Why did Mr Catherick leave the village forever?
4 Why did Sir Percival put Anne in the Asylum?
5 Why did Walter Hartright go and see Mrs Catherick?
6 What difference did Walter Hartright find between the vestry register and the copy Mr Wansborough had kept?
7 How did Sir Percival die?
8 What was Sir Percival's secret?

Grammar

2 **Complete the sentences with the correct question tag.**

Mrs Clements was very fond of Anne Catherick, *wasn't she* ?
1 Something strange happened to Mrs Clements, _____ ?
2 Mrs Catherick didn't love her husband, _____ ?
3 Mr Catherick had seen his wife with Sir Percival, _____ ?
4 Mrs Catherick tells Walter Hartright to go away, _____ ?
5 The man in the vestry should look after things better, _____ ?
6 Walter will tell Marian everything, _____ ?
7 Walter would like to know the name of Anne Catherick's father, _____ ?

Writing

3 **You're Walter Hartright. Write a letter to Marian (about 100 words). In the letter you should:**

- explain what you found in the register and the copy
- describe how Sir Percival died and explain his secret

Vocabulary

4 Complete the sentences with the correct word from the box.

> too • such • many • much • ~~quite~~ • very • enough • so

Sandon was ___quite___ far from Blackwater Park.
1 Mrs Clements told the Count that Anne Catherick was _____ ill to travel.
2 Walter Hartright didn't spend _____ time with Mrs Catherick when he visited her.
3 The Count was _____ a clever man that he had organised the crime perfectly.
4 Mrs Catherick was _____ angry with Sir Percival for what he had done to her.
5 How _____ gifts did Sir Percival give Mrs Catherick when she was young?
6 Sir Percival wasn't strong _____ to open the vestry door.
7 After the fire, Walter Hartright was _____ tired that he sat on the ground.

PRE-READING ACTIVITY

Listening

▶ 12 **5 Listen to the start of Chapter Eight and circle the correct word(s) to make true sentences.**

William Hartright got another letter from Marian *(before)/after* leaving for London.
1 In the letter, Marian *explained/didn't explain* why she had moved house.
2 Walter Hartright arrived in London that *night/morning*.
3 Marian and Laura were both *ill/well*.
4 Marian had seen Count Fosco *the day before/the week before*.
5 The Count sent Marian a *card/note*.
6 The Count waited for Marian *at the Asylum/in the street*.

79

Chapter 8

Count Fosco's Past Life

▶ 12 Before leaving for London, I got another letter from Marian. She said they had moved house but didn't say why. I was worried. I got the first train to London and went to their new address. It was dark when I arrived. Both Marian and Laura were well. After Laura had gone to bed, Marian told me why they had come to their new rooms in Fulham.

'I saw Count Fosco yesterday,' said Marian, 'and worse than that, Walter – I spoke to him. He came to our house. Luckily, Laura never saw him. I saw him from the window at first. He was with the doctor of the Asylum. They spoke for a bit then the owner of the Asylum went away. The Count sent a card up to me asking me to speak to him, so I went downstairs and met him in the street. He said if we do anything against him, he'll tell the doctor of the Asylum that Laura is here. That's why I decided to move to Fulham.'

'Don't worry, Marian,' I said. 'I'm well-prepared for Count Fosco. We'll wait and he'll think we have listened to him. When he feels safe, he'll make a mistake. Now, though, you must tell Laura that Sir Percival is dead.'

Marian told Laura the next morning. I found a better-paid job because we needed more money to rent this house. It was now December and I had found out that Count Fosco had decided to stay in London until the end of June of the following year.

I still wanted to know who Anne Catherick's father was. I wrote to Major Donthorne, of Varneck Hall where Mrs Catherick had worked as a servant for some years before her marriage. Two days later, he wrote back saying that Sir Percival Glyde had never come to Varneck Hall. Instead, Mr Philip Fairlie, of Limmeridge House, had been a great friend of Major Donthorne and had often stayed there. He had found some old letters and could say for sure that Mr Philip Fairlie had stayed at Varneck Hall from August to October 1826.

We knew that Mrs Catherick had been there at the same time, and that Anne was born in June 1827. Anne had always looked like Laura, and Laura was very like her father. Mr Philip Fairlie had been a very popular, handsome man. In fact, Mrs Catherick had said that Mrs Fairlie had married the most handsome man in England. It was now obvious that Anne's father had been Mr Philip Fairlie. Did he ever know? Did Mrs Fairlie ever know? Marian didn't think so.

April came. I was earning well and Laura seemed more like her old self. However, she still couldn't remember everything. Apart from that, she was like the old Laura I had loved and we were both once more in love with each other. We decided to go on holiday to the beach for two weeks. After the third day, I spoke to Marian about Laura. We agreed that if we wanted Count Fosco to pay for his crime, it would be better if I married Laura. I could protect her more easily this way. Sir Percival had spent all Laura's money, so now I, a poor drawing teacher, could ask her to be my wife. Ten days later, we were married.

We returned to London happier than ever, but still with a problem to solve. We had to find a way of making the Count admit to what he had done, in writing, if we wanted people to believe that Laura was really Laura and still alive. This was the only way, because Laura still couldn't remember what had happened to her in London. The Count was the only one who could tell us the exact date Laura had travelled to London. If this date was after the 25th July, the date that Anne Catherick had died, then everybody would know the truth at last.

It was now the beginning of May, so we had to move fast before the Count left his house in June. I was afraid he might leave the country. I needed to know more about Count Fosco so I arranged to go to the theatre with my old Italian friend, Mr Pesca. I knew Count Fosco would be there. We found seats far from the Count but near enough for Pesca to see his face.

'No,' said Pesca, looking at the Count, 'I've never seen that man before.'

Just as he was saying these words, the Count looked up and saw Mr Pesca. The Count's face changed. It was obvious that the Count knew Pesca, and he was afraid of him. Near us, there was a tall, slim man and he too was looking at Fosco and had noticed the change in him.

'He definitely knows you,' I said to Pesca.

The Count got up to leave. The tall, slim man left too. We tried to follow them but there was a crowd and we lost them.

I took Pesca home and explained the situation to him.

'He knows you, Pesca,' I said. 'He's afraid of you – there must be a reason. Think back to the time when you still lived in Italy.'

Pesca suddenly seemed very frightened. He walked up and down the room for a moment then said:

'You saved my life once, Walter. My next words will put my life into your hands. When I was in Italy, I belonged to a society. Let's call it 'The Brotherhood'. The members of this society don't know each other. Only the heads of the society for each country, and their secretaries know who the members are. We live a normal life but four times a year, we must go to the society and offer our services. If we betray* The Brotherhood, they kill us. While I was still in Italy, I was secretary of the society, so I saw all the members face to face. Look at this red circle on my arm, Walter. This is the sign of The Brotherhood and every member has this sign. If the man at the theatre knows me, he is so changed that I don't recognise him, and if he's afraid of me, it means that he has betrayed The Brotherhood.'

I was sure the Count would want to leave London that night. I had to move fast. First, I went home and wrote a letter to Pesca, which said:

The man at the theatre is a member of The Brotherhood. He has betrayed this society. His name in England is Count Fosco and he lives at no.5 Forest Road, St. John's Wood. As my friend, do all you can against this man. I have done everything I could and have lost all and paid for it with my life.

I signed and put the date on the letter. On the outside, I wrote: *'Do not open this letter until nine o'clock tomorrow morning. If you don't hear from me or see me, read it.'* Then I sent it to Pesca. It was now eleven o'clock, time to go to Count Fosco's. When I got there, the tall, slim man from the theatre was walking past Fosco's house but he didn't stop and go in. I rang the bell and a servant showed me into a room where the Count was sitting surrounded by his things. He was obviously preparing to leave London.

'What business brings you here?' asked the Count.

'I see you're preparing to leave London,' I said, 'and I know why. Let me see your arm.'

The Count stood up, locked the door and went towards his gun on the desk.

'Wait,' I said. 'There's a note you might like to see.'

betray give information about a person, group or your country, to the enemy

It was a note from Pesca saying that he had received my letter and that he'd open it if he didn't see me by nine o'clock the next morning. The Count understood what it meant.

'What do you want from me,' he asked.

'I'm here for my wife's interests. First, you must write what you did and sign it. Second, you must tell me the exact date my wife left Blackwater Park, and travelled to London.'

'I'll do what you want if you do as I ask,' said the Count. 'I have a letter from Sir Percival telling me the day and time of his wife's arrival in London, signed, with the date – that's what you need, isn't it? However, first, Madame Fosco and I leave this house, when and how we want. Second, you wait here with me to see my lawyer, who's coming at seven o'clock tomorrow morning. You give my lawyer a note telling the man who's got your letter to give it to him and bring it here. You wait here until I have that letter in my hands, then you allow me half an hour to leave this house, and then you can go wherever you want.'

'I agree to everything,' I said, 'but only if you destroy the letter in front of me as soon as you get it.'

The Count agreed and sat at his desk to write down what he had done.

He finished writing at four o'clock. Then he gave me Sir Percival's letter. It said: 'Hampshire, 25th July', and told the Count that Lady Glyde would travel to London on the 26th. So, on the day written on the death certificate, she was still alive at Blackwater Park and the day after, she was going to travel to London.

The lawyer, Mr Rubelle, came at seven o'clock, went to get the letter from Pesca, and came straight back. The Count immediately burnt the letter in front of me, and then he left with his wife. I waited

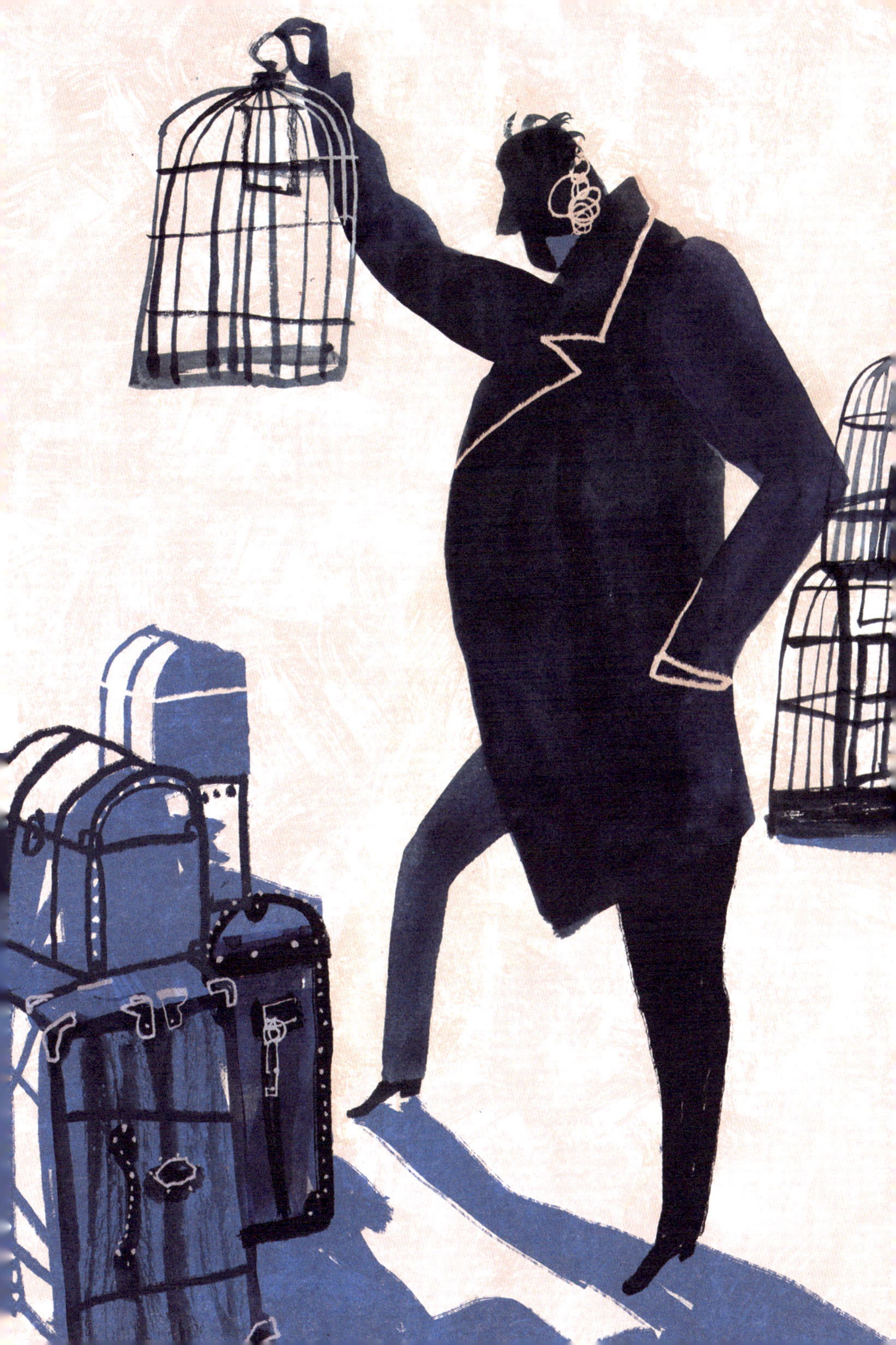

with Mr Rubelle for half an hour, then I left with the Count's letter safely in my bag.

When I got home, I read the Count's story. Of course, I already knew most of it. The only thing that had spoiled his plan was that the false Lady Glyde had died before the true Lady Glyde arrived in London on 26th July. After giving her something to make her sleep, they had dressed Lady Glyde in Anne Catherick's clothes and had taken her to the Asylum on the 27th in the evening.

The next day, I left with Laura, Marian and the lawyer, Mr Kyrle, for Limmeridge. I spoke to Mr Fairlie with Mr Kyrle. He was, as usual, only worried about himself. He agreed to have a meeting with the local people at Limmeridge House the next day, to tell them that his niece, Laura, was alive.

The day came. Everybody stood up when Marian and I led Laura into Limmeridge House. Mr Fairlie and Mr Kyrle were there too. I explained to everybody what had happened. I then told them that Sir Percival was dead and that Laura was now my wife.

'Do you all agree,' I asked the crowd, pointing to my wife, 'that this is Laura?'

'Everybody cried, 'Yes!' and started clapping and shouting. They were all so happy to see Laura again.

That evening, Mr Fairlie sent me a letter – he was too tired to speak – asking if we were going to stay at Limmeridge. I wrote back that he needn't worry. He wouldn't see or hear from us again. Then, the three of us went to the station and returned to London to start our new life together.

Shortly after, the newspaper I worked for sent me to Paris for a few days. It was there that I discovered that Fosco was dead. Pesca told me that Fosco had died at the hands of the tall, slim man who had been at the theatre. I went to see his body. There was a knife through his heart and I saw the red circle on his arm. Somebody had written the letter 'T' over the circle – T for traitor*. They never found the tall, slim man but The Brotherhood had found Count Fosco.

Madame Fosco buried him in France and puts fresh flowers on his grave every day. She wrote a book about her husband but we'll never know his real name.

I returned to London. The following year, our first child was born – a son. When our little Walter was six months old, something happened. At that time, I was in Ireland for work for two weeks. When I returned, I found out that Laura, Marian and the child had gone to Limmeridge House. I went straight there. I found them in the room where I used to draw.

'What has brought you here?' I asked.

'Mr Fairlie is dead,' said Marian, 'and little Walter is the new owner of Limmeridge!'

And with these last words from Marian, my story ends.

traitor a person who goes against his group or country by helping the enemy

AFTER-READING ACTIVITIES

Stop & Check

1 **Choose the correct answer, A, B or C about Chapter Eight.**

Count Fosco had decided to stay in London
- A̶ until the end of June.
- B until the end of July.
- C until the end of August.

1 In his letter, Major Donthorne said
- A Sir Percival Glyde had been his friend.
- B Sir Percival Glyde had never stayed at his home.
- C Sir Percival Glyde had written him lots of letters.

2 Mr Philip Fairlie had stayed at Varneck Hall
- A from June 1826 to October 1826.
- B from August 1826 to June 1827.
- C from August 1826 to October 1826.

3 Sir Percival had
- A saved all Laura's money.
- B spent all Laura's money.
- C given all Laura's money to the Count.

4 Mr Pesca saw the Count
- A at home.
- B in the street.
- C at the theatre.

5 When Walter arrived at Fosco's house, the Count was
- A talking to his lawyer.
- B playing with his mice.
- C getting ready to leave.

6 When the Count got Pesca's letter,
- A he burnt it.
- B he took it with him.
- C he gave it to his wife.

7 Fosco was killed by
- A Walter Hartright.
- B the stranger at the theatre.
- C Mr Pesca.

Writing

2 Write about Marian, Laura, Anne Catherick, Mrs Catherick and Madame Fosco. Talk about:

- their character
- how important they are for the story
- what you liked or didn't like about them.

Marian: _____
_____
_____

Laura: _____
_____
_____

Anne Catherick: _____
_____
_____

Mrs Catherick: _____
_____
_____

Madame Fosco: _____
_____

Vocabulary

3 All these words are in the glossary. How many of them can you remember? Match each word to the correct definition.

1. ☐ Asylum
2. ☐ uneasy
3. ☐ betray
4. ☐ spy
5. ☐ debts
6. ☐ confirm
7. ☐ guardian
8. ☐ delicate
9. ☐ property

a not strong, easy to break.
b hospital for the care of mentally ill people.
c say something is true.
d a person, who by law, takes care of a young person.
e land and buildings that belong to a person.
f give information about somebody to an enemy.
g a person who listens and watches in secret.
h not happy, worried.
i money you must pay to others.

FOCUS ON...

Wilkie Collins (1824-1889)

William Wilkie Collins was an English writer and one of his most famous books is *The Woman in White* written in 1859. Wilkie Collins himself, considered this his best book, but he also wrote other books, three of which are *No Name* (1862), *Armadale* (1866) and *The Moonstone* (1868) as well as short stories and plays. On his gravestone, you can read the words: '*William Wilkie Collins (1824-1889) Author of The Woman in White and other works of fiction.*' *The Woman in White* is one of the first and best of the '*sensation novels*' which were very popular in Great Britain in the 1860s and 1870s. These books were similar to '*gothic fiction*' where there was always a secret to discover, but they were more frightening because they were closer to real life. In *The Woman in White*, realistic characters tell a mysterious story in a real life setting*.

Early Life

Collins was born in Marylebone, an area in central London. His father was a well-known landscape painter, William Collins, and his mother was called Harriet Geddes. The family moved to Hampstead, another part of London, in 1826 and his brother, Charles was born there. Their mother taught the two boys at home when they were young. Then in 1835, Wilkie Collins went to school at the Maida Vale Academy. For two years, from 1836 to 1838, he lived in Italy and France with his family and learnt to speak both Italian and French. Then the family returned to England and he went to school in Highbury. While he was there, he discovered that he was good at telling stories and he decided he wanted to continue along this path once he left school in 1840. However, his father found him a job with a company that bought and sold tea. Collins didn't like this job, but he stayed there for over five years. During this time Collins wrote some stories but they weren't very successful. Then, in 1846, his father decided to send Wilkie to *Lincoln's Inn* to study to be a lawyer. Wilkie Collins wasn't really interested and didn't finish his studies until 1851, when he eventually became a lawyer. However, he used this knowledge in many of the books he wrote.

setting where a story happens

Wilkie Collins and Charles Dickens

In 1851, Wilkie Collins met Charles Dickens for the first time. They became lifetime friends and worked together. Wilkie Collins wrote the story, *A Terribly Strange Bed* for Dickens' weekly magazine called *Household Words* in 1852. He also went on tour with Dickens' company of actors. Unfortunately, Collins began to suffer from gout, a very painful illness that stayed with him for the rest of his life. When he was feeling better, he travelled around many places in Europe with his friend Dickens. Wilkie Collins' story *The Woman in White* first appeared weekly, in Dickens' magazine *All the Year Round* and the ordinary people loved it, even if the newspapers didn't seem so keen on it. Sales of the magazine grew as every week, people waited to read what had happened in the story.

(From left) Charles Dickens Jr., Kate Dickens, Charles Dickens, Miss Hogarth, Mary Dickens, Wilkie Collins

The Woman in White

Some people say that Collins got his idea for the first meeting between William Hartright and the Woman in White of his book, from something that happened to him in real life. It's said that Wilkie was walking home in London one night with friends, when a girl dressed in white came running out of a house. His friends did nothing but Wilkie followed this woman to see if he could help her. Many believe that this woman was Caroline Graves and this was how they first met. Caroline was a young woman, in her early twenties with a daughter. By now, Collins was thirty-two. He decided to go and live with Caroline, but didn't marry her. Apart from a short period when Caroline married a plumber and then left him after a few years, Collins stayed with her and her daughter for the rest of his life. He also had another woman in his life, Martha Rudd and they had three children. When he died, these two women he had shared his life with, each got half of his money.

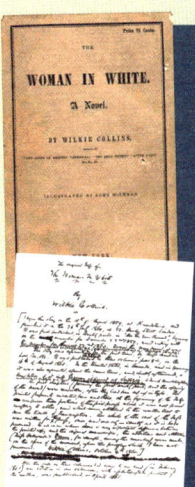

Task

Complete this form about Wilkie Collins.

Born   _____
Place of Birth   _____
Father's job   _____
Most famous books   _____
Friend and colleague   _____
Women he loved   _____
Died   _____

FOCUS ON...

CLIL History

Women in the Victorian Age

When describing Laura's feelings about her marriage to Sir Percival Glyde, Marian says:
She doesn't love her future husband. Her father made her promise on his death-bed two years ago. Till you came here, she was the same as hundreds of other women, who marry men without liking or disliking them, and who learn to love or hate them after marriage.

So, what was life like for women in this period? In the Victorian Age, they believed that a woman's duty was to keep the house clean for her husband, put food on the table and give him children. When a woman got married, her husband controlled any money and property she had except for land property. Women lost all control over any property they brought into the marriage, even following divorce. A husband also had complete control over any money his wife earned from her property. Women were not allowed to keep their own money in a bank and a married woman couldn't sign any documents without her husband agreeing.

Both single and married women had many disadvantages in society compared to men. Men had all the power and it was very difficult for women to escape from an unhappy marriage. Even if their husbands went with other women, the wife often stayed in this situation because she had no money of her own.

However, in the upper classes the duties of a woman to manage a house full of servants was considered an important part of Victorian life. The husband was still head of the family but his wife took care of the organisation of the house, from paying the servants and bills to educating their children. The woman of the house also had to organise dinners and parties to make sure her husband was part of the important social circles of that time. During the Victorian Age, many books giving advice about running a successful home and the duties of an ideal wife were very popular among the middle classes.

The Working Classes

Life for a working-class family in the Victorian Age was far less comfortable. Houses were often old and let the rain in, so a working-class mother had to do her best to keep her family as clean, warm and dry as possible. London was full of families living in single rooms. These women had no servants and had to do all the cleaning, cooking and washing. The air in London was full of the smoke from factories that made everything black and dirty. Many working-class women also worked to bring some more money into the family. They did hard jobs like working in the fields. Then with the Industrial Revolution, they began working in factories.

Education

If they had the chance, women of a higher social class usually studied subjects like history, geography and literature so that they would have interesting things to talk about during social events. Very few women studied subjects like physics, science or engineering and very few went to university. Some people even said it was against a woman's nature to study and could even make her ill.

Change

In the middle of the 19th century, they started to introduce new laws to help women. In 1857, a woman could finally get a divorce if her husband was cruel to her and in 1870, a new law said that women could keep the money they earned for themselves. These changes and many others meant that if she wanted, a woman could now leave her husband as she had her own money to live on.

Task – Internet Search

Have a look on the Internet. Find out more about the Victorian Age.

- Where does it get its name from?
- What was important for the people of this Age?
- What did the British think of people from other countries?
- What was happening in science at this time?

TEST YOURSELF

Choose A, B or C to complete the sentences about *The Woman in White*.

William Hartright first met the woman in white
- **A** in London. ✓
- **B** in Cumberland.
- **C** in Hampshire.

1. Mr Philip Fairlie was
   - **A** Laura's uncle.
   - **B** Laura's cousin.
   - **C** Laura's father.

2. Laura Fairlie got married
   - **A** before her 21st birthday.
   - **B** on her 21st birthday.
   - **C** after her 21st birthday.

3. On her 21st birthday, Miss Fairlie would get
   - **A** £5000.
   - **B** £10,000.
   - **C** £20,000.

4. Sir Percival Glyde wanted Lady Glyde
   - **A** to go back to Limmeridge.
   - **B** to send Marian away.
   - **C** to sign a document.

5. Laura met Anne Catherick
   - **A** at the boat-house.
   - **B** in Welmingham.
   - **C** in London.

6. Marian needed help so she wrote to her lawyer and
   - **A** Mr Fairlie.
   - **B** Mr Hartright.
   - **C** Mr Pesca.

7. When Fanny woke up, she found the letters
   - **A** in her pocket.
   - **B** near the bed.
   - **C** on the table.

8. Mrs Catherick had been a servant at
   - **A** Limmeridge House.
   - **B** Blackwater Park.
   - **C** Varneck Hall.

9. Anne Catherick was born in
   - **A** May 1827.
   - **B** June 1827.
   - **C** July 1827.

10. Sir Felix didn't marry Sir Percival's mother because
    - **A** she ran away with another man.
    - **B** he didn't love her.
    - **C** she was already married.

11. Anne Catherick's father was
    - **A** Count Fosco.
    - **B** Philip Fairlie.
    - **C** Sir Percival Glyde.

12. Count Fosco was killed in
    - **A** London.
    - **B** Paris.
    - **C** Italy.

SYLLABUS

Level B1

This reader contains the items listed below as well as those included in previous levels of the ELI Readers syllabus.

Verb Tenses
Present Perfect Simple
Past Perfect Simple

Verb Forms and Patterns
make/let + infinitive
Verb + object + infinitive (e.g. I want you to help)
Reported speech with say, ask, tell.
Phrasal verbs
had better

Modal Verbs
can / could
may / might
should / ought to
must / have to
need / needn't
used to

Clauses
Time clauses introduced by when, while, until, before, after...
Clauses of purpose
First conditional
Second conditional
Clauses of concession

YOUNG ADULT ELI READERS

STAGE 1
Jonathan Swift, *Gulliver's Travels*
Sir Arthur Conan Doyle, *The Hound of the Baskervilles*
Daniel Defoe, *Robinson Crusoe*
Sir Arthur Conan Doyle, *A Study in Scarlet*

STAGE 2
Charles Dickens, *Great Expectations*
William Shakespeare, *Romeo and Juliet*
Bram Stoker, *Dracula*
William Shakespeare, *A Midsummer Night's Dream*
Robert Louis Stevenson, *The Strange Case of Dr Jekyll and Mr Hyde*
Jerome K. Jerome, *Three Men in a Boat*
William Shakespeare, *Hamlet*

STAGE 3
Charlotte Brontë, *Jane Eyre*
Jane Austen, *Pride and Prejudice*
Oscar Wilde, *The Picture of Dorian Gray*
William Shakespeare, *Macbeth*
Jane Austen, *Sense and Sensibility*
Edith Wharton, *The Age of Innocence*
Wilkie Collins, *The Woman in White*
Henry James, *The Portrait of a Lady*

STAGE 4
James Joyce, *Dubliners*
Mary Shelley, *Frankenstein*
Henry James, *The Turn of the Screw*
Emily Brontë, *Wuthering Heights*
Edgar Allan Poe, *Stories of Mystery and Suspense*
Charles and Mary Lamb, *Tales from Shakespeare*
Charles Dickens, *A Tale of Two Cities*
Anthony Hope, *The Prisoner of Zenda*
Hermann Melville, *Moby Dick*

STAGE 5
Virginia Woolf, *Mrs Dalloway*
Francis Scott Fitzgerald, *The Great Gatsby*
William Makepeace Thackeray, *Vanity Fair*

STAGE 6
Joseph Conrad, *Heart of Darkness*
J. Borsbey & R. Swan, Editors, *A Collection of First World War Poetry*
Oscar Wilde, *The Importance of Being Earnest*

YOUNG ADULT ELI READERS LIGHT

Edgar Allan Poe, *The Narrative of Arthur Gordon Pym of Nantucket*

Natsume Sōseki, *Botchan*